The
SUCCESSFUL
MUMPRENEUR

HOW TO WORK FLEXIBLY
AROUND YOUR FAMILY
DOING WHAT YOU LOVE

DEBBIE GILBERT

MUMPRENEUR SINCE 1998

The Successful Mumpreneur

First published in 2018 by

Panoma Press Ltd
48 St Vincent Drive, St Albans, Herts, AL1 5SJ, UK
info@panomapress.com
www.panomapress.com

Book layout by Neil Coe.

Printed on acid-free paper from managed forests.

ISBN 978-1-784521-44-8

TESTIMONIALS

As a mother of three boys and owner of a business, I wish this book existed when I was starting out. It is an honest account of why so many women choose self-employment over a corporate career, what to expect when starting and growing a business, and how to do it without sacrificing time with those we love. The book is a nonsense-free zone full of practical advice. A must-read for women who love the idea of running their own business, or simply want to become better at it.

Lenka Lutonska MABNLP, TLTA, MABH, Managing Director & Principal Coach at LenkaLutonska.com

I have read the whole book and I love it. I think it is just the right mix of advice, how to's and personal stories. With this sort of book, the thing that I struggle with is all the 'blah blah blah' which makes the book really long but doesn't add any value. This book doesn't have any of this – it's straight to the point and doesn't waffle. It's easy to read and enjoyable (because of the personal stories) as well as informative.

Cheryl Luzet, CEO, Wagada

FOREWORD

What is parenting? According to Wikipedia 'Parenting is the process of promoting and supporting the physical, emotional, social and intellectual development of a child from infancy to adulthood.'

The word that rings out to me from that definition is 'supporting'; I think my Mum has perfectly encapsulated this word in my childhood because for the last 16 years I have felt constantly supported.

When I say that my Mum is a very successful businesswoman who runs several different businesses, people initially think that I've had a neglected childhood; as if my Mum hasn't been there and has left me in childcare. I can tell you that nothing could be further from the truth.

I honestly believe that my mother has created an incredible environment for me to thrive and develop in. I would even go as far as to say that her being a very successful independent businesswoman is what has really enabled her to give me what has been an unquestionably remarkable childhood.

You see, I speak to you as a 16-year-old who has done some amazing things with his life that so many other kids would be lucky to have done so young. I've been on fantastic holidays to all sorts of interesting places, including riding a camel on Christmas Day in Morocco! We couldn't have done those things without her ability to create this life as a successful entrepreneur.

When I look back over my childhood, I've had the opportunity to do so many extracurricular activities. I've attended a performing arts academy since I was five, had regular appearances in youth shows, I play rugby for my local team, learned to play drums and so it goes on. And the reason I get to do all these things is because my Mum has the money and the time to support me. I wouldn't change it for the world.

I understand there are many kids who haven't had what I have because their mums or dads work such long hours that they just simply don't have the time. It doesn't mean that they don't love their kids, it just means that they are living a different lifestyle. I've been incredibly lucky to have a mother who supports me in everything that I do, having made the time to be there when I needed her.

She made a huge sacrifice for me when I was given the life-changing opportunity to be cast in a West End show. I played Augustus Gloop in the original cast of *Charlie and the Chocolate Factory* and that of course required a huge investment of her time. I know that if my Mum hadn't worked for herself she would never have been able to make it happen for me. We're not talking about a small commitment here, we're talking about taking me to rehearsals every day. Driving into London, late nights after the show, helping me learn my script and supporting me with school work.

Because my Mum worked for herself she was able to adapt her working life, so she could be there for me. This doesn't mean that she didn't work, it simply means she just found another way, because her working life enabled her to. Whether it be going to a business centre in London or a bustling café and just working or meeting contacts while I was rehearsing, my Mum somehow found a way to balance her work with mine. And she made it look easy!

There's not been one moment in my childhood where I thought my Mum hasn't been there for me. She really has been a constant source of support throughout my childhood. She's been at every school play I've been in, every rugby match I've ever played, every show I've ever done and every other waking moment where a child wants his mum cheering him on. It's been my Mum's mission to come to every parents' evening and take huge levels of responsibility for my learning and progression. I remember as a small child having my mother help me with my homework as soon as I got through the door. This was a privilege that I definitely took for granted.

A good childhood relies on the little things, like sitting and watching television together, walking the dogs, going food shopping (me constantly asking for stuff I didn't need!), or even reading a book together. My Mum isn't dictated to by the demands of the corporate world. She works incredibly hard but she's her own boss, and personally, I wouldn't have it any other way. She's an incredibly strong person who I admire and respect to the highest degree. I believe it's an amazing thing that she got to raise her children whilst running a business when traditionally women have either focused on their careers or their kids. There's often no crossover or in-between, it's either one or the other.

I think my Mum has made a massive success of her life, all whilst creating an incredible bond with her children. She's guaranteed her independence and I think it's a credit to her and to any other woman that chooses to make that leap into the unknown territory of becoming a Mumpreneur. I hope this book helps and encourages parents to follow suit. If you do, you have a great opportunity to become a success in business and as a mum.

I am a happy teenager, a very rare thing these days, and that is because of the amazing 16 years I've had on this wonderful planet Earth. I am incredibly proud of my Mum because she is an inspiration to all who know her.

This book has allowed her to bless the masses with her immense knowledge and experience that she has on the subject of being both a successful businesswoman and a very successful mother.

This is my opportunity to thank her for everything and tell her how incredibly proud I am to call her my Mum.

Regan Stokes
Son of Deborah Gilbert

CONTENTS

INTRODUCTION

Why read this book?

Congratulations if you are thinking of starting a business – you will find from this book that you are not alone!

A Mumpreneur is someone who starts a business to work around their children. Escalating childcare costs and commuting stresses have seen a huge increase in women quitting the 9 to 5 employment to set up businesses from home while looking after their children.

As you are reading this book I am hoping you have some interest in finding out what it takes to run your own business as a parent. This is an invaluable guide, using my own experiences and those of trusted experts I know, about working for yourself around a family to make an income. It also shares the experiences of other Mumpreneurs.

A business for you might be a full-time income, whilst for others it will be about having some financial independence whilst balancing the needs of your family.

Working for a company as an employee has many benefits. It's important to consider these when deciding to work for yourself. You get a pension scheme, holiday and sick pay, maternity leave, possibly a benefits package, contact with people daily, maybe training and further development and a daily structure.

The downsides if you have a family will include:

- Childcare costs

- Inflexible working patterns – there are 13 weeks' school holidays and you will probably get four or five weeks' holiday

- The working day usually starts at 9 and finishes around 5 – school hours are 8.45am-3pm

- Schools usually have assemblies, sports days, plays and various activities during the school day and if you are working you may not be able to get the time off

- If your child is sick you may have to pretend to be!

I found working full time around my son very stressful and after two and a half years decided it wasn't for me. I recognised that I would need a long-term solution that allowed me to balance work and parenting.

It was important to me to spend as much time as possible with my child. I wanted to be at the school gates at the end of the day, to nurse him when he was sick, to be at the front row of every school performance and sports day. Because in my view this wasn't going to be forever, it was a very short space of time. I also had a family who needed my help and support.

Many people see working for themselves as an easy option. It isn't. However, there are several reasons why parents start a business and the main one is to have more time to be with their children.

So, when you think about why you want to work for yourself really think quite deeply into it and at your reasons. Giving up a job with all the security it offers may not be the right option for you. However, working for yourself can also fill a gap. You might not want to do it forever, but you may find this is your ideal life and is what you want. I personally could never go back to working full time for an employer.

Why I work for myself

In 1998 I began working for myself after becoming a single parent when my son was three. I left corporate life as I wanted to work part time to spend more time with him. However, other than retail, part-time jobs were almost non-existent. In 1998 the internet was in its infancy, mobile phones only offered short text messages and there were not many mums working for themselves, except for Tupperware and Avon! Few people had heard of business networking.

I never planned to have a business. Things evolved over time. In some ways things were simpler then but in other ways much harder. For example, it was harder to reach the target market and communication was much clunkier.

Mistakes – well, being honest I will admit I have made a few! But I think it's more constructive to highlight the differences between today and 20 years ago. Technology really does make it easier for you to start a business now.

In 2007 I decided to start my own networking group as I recognised I wanted more contacts and I needed to widen my network, so I bought a franchise, and I will talk more about this later in the book. As you will read, it didn't work out for me with the franchisor, but I continued the business I had built and rebranded in 2009. I then started Mums UnLtd in 2011, a company that provides networking and support for mums in business.

A lot of what I share with you in this book comes from the insights of Mumpreneurs, the mistakes they have made and the things they did to succeed.

Let me say to you that your business, the one you are planning right now in your head, probably won't be the business you will have in two years' time. Your ideas will grow and develop through the experiences you have and the people you meet. There will be changes in the marketplace and you will need to learn to be able to adapt quickly and diversify to be successful.

I have written this book as a business companion, something you can dip in and out of for ideas, motivation and inspiration. Whether you're thinking about starting a business or you've already taken the plunge, this book is designed to be able to help you get things right as much as possible.

This book will help you navigate your way through the minefield of running a business. It has been deliberately designed to take you through a structured process – so try and work through each stage and subject in order.

I have had some amazing input from other Mumpreneurs who are sharing their stories, expert tips and advice in this book. Thousands of women now work around their family, so you are not alone. There will be support in your local area. Plus you can use this book to learn from the experiences of others and think about how you can apply them to your life.

Running a business isn't for everyone. It's not the easy solution to a way out of the 9 to 5 routine, but it can have tremendous rewards for you, your clients and above all your family.

Good luck on your journey. I am so pleased that by buying this book you are taking me with you. Please do share your thoughts, questions and experiences with me. My contact details are at the back of the book. I cannot wait to hear about your business!

Best wishes
Debbie Gilbert

STAGE ONE

Chapter 1

WHY DO YOU WANT TO WORK FOR YOURSELF?

In this chapter I want you to take some time to consider your options and make a very well-informed decision about starting a business. I will go through some of my thoughts about the pros and cons of being self-employed. Having worked full time juggling the needs of my son in corporate life (I went back full time when he was just 17 weeks old) and having run a business now for over 20 years (he was three when I started the business), I feel well qualified to share these with you. By the end of this chapter you will be able to review your personal circumstances and make a well thought out decision.

You cannot start a successful business instantly!

Getting a business up and running takes time, commitment and usually some funding. It may also take a while to see a regular income coming in. Think about how you will live, what income you need (and have access to) to support yourself (i.e. savings or other income).

Also, consider this:

Employment = paid regular salary, paid holidays, sick pay and potentially other benefits

Self-Employment = Payment on sale of goods or services and no benefits

This is the stark reality. Too many mums start a business thinking it will be easier than working for an employer.

It isn't easier, it's different.

Failure in business startups is huge, around 80% in the first three years and it's just as high in the next three years.

What's more common? Someone who runs a business making virtually no money, or as I like to call it an expensive hobby! What separates the successful Mumpreneur from an unsuccessful one? The successful ones get advice, support and then *listen.* They research their idea carefully, work on the numbers and work out a strategy to combine this with their family. Then, most importantly of all, they execute their strategy.

Consider this:

You automatically have two jobs once you have a child.

Mumpreneur was a term coined a few years ago as more mums began to start a business. But actually, when you think about it, mums have been Mumpreneurs for centuries. This is nothing new, we just have a name for it now.

So, we are combining an Entrepreneur: 'a person who sets up a business or businesses, taking on financial risks in the hope of profit'

With Mum (Mother): 'a woman in relation to her child or children, bringing up (a child) with care and affection'.

Being an entrepreneur is already a hard, long road. Then we add in a second job – raising a family. Here lies the problem!

Most women start a business doing something they know already but what they don't know is how to run a business or how to do it whilst balancing the needs of a family. And new mothers are finding their way around parenthood too!

So just for a moment I would like you to STOP and work through the following questions:

S – Structure Think about the structure of your life.

How many children do you have?

How many do you plan to have?

How much support can you count on?

T – Time

How much child-free time do you have?

How much can you create?

O – Opportunities and Options

What opportunities can you create for a business?

What options do you have?

P – Planning – Proper Planning Prevents Pathetic Performance!

I cannot remember where I heard this, but it has stuck with me for years. And it is so true. So, if you go down the self-employed route you need to start writing the business and marketing plans. They will help you to see where your gaps are.

We have lots of information in this book on what you need to do, including business plans and marketing plans.

Your Pros and Cons list

If you are like me, you hate writing in books! So, take a sheet of paper and let's explore what working for yourself might mean to you. Write a list, draw a mind map and explore your thoughts and write them down with whichever method works for you. You need to identify a pros and cons list for staying in employment versus becoming self-employed.

Pros list – items might include:

- Full-time salary – reliable income

- Benefits package – what is the total value of all non-salary extras e.g. bonus scheme, life insurance, childcare vouchers etc.

- Company car, healthcare, pension

- Structure – times you work, and holiday time is structured

- Paid holiday

- Sick pay

- Interaction with colleagues

- Doing a job you have trained for/love

Cons of starting a business vs staying employed – might include:

- Expensive childcare

- No benefits

- No structure

- No paid holiday

- No sick pay

- No colleagues to interact with

- Problems when children are sick

- You may require training

Common reasons why mums work for themselves

Let's share some stories from women who turned to self-employment

- **Employers refuse flexible working**

Yuliana Topazly - My OutSpace Business Centre

I had a job which I enjoyed doing, however after getting married and giving birth to my lovely daughter Jessica, my employer refused my rights of flexible working, so I had to find an alternative. I wanted to spend more time with her and childcare provisions were so expensive. I made the decision to leave as this, combined with the fact I did not see my daughter most of the week, made working full time no longer possible. I decided to review how I could use my existing skills. During this time, I met with several other mothers who were struggling with the work/life balance.

So, I decided to create a child-friendly working and support environment. My OutSpace is a centre that provides flexible workspace alongside high-quality business support tailored to the needs of female entrepreneurs. Workspace has a lot of potential although it takes a lot of hard work and it is localised. My aim is to support as many parents who are struggling in silence as possible. I have now developed an online platform www.buddywith.org.uk, which helps parents to connect depending on the issues they may face and the support they need. It is free to use and offers a buddying up service, has a pool of resources and access to various support organisations.

• I want to spend more time with my children

Bess Sturman - Sturman & Co. Interior Design

I started my business after I had my third child. I left a successful corporate and legal career. It had always been my dream to design interiors, furniture or buildings and I felt there would never be a better time to be creative. As a full-time head of department at a major healthcare company, I had loved my job, but my role as mum of three felt as if it was being slowly stolen from me. I was grabbing at short spells of time with my children, often taking conference calls or writing emails while I was with them, so I could carry out my job properly. I wanted a life where my children and home were central to everything and I could dictate my own hours and work.

When I started the business, I was in a real hurry to be a success. I really had to force myself to slow down at times, to enjoy the time I was getting with my children and do only what was achievable. When I look back on it, the time I had with my little babies was so short; I sometimes regret I didn't give myself even more space to enjoy them. I could have slowed down my business journey until the youngest had reached two years old.

My family priorities are to be there for my children and listen to them at the end of every school day. I also want to be the kind of mum who engages with my children and inspires them to take opportunities.

Your family and your wellbeing must be your priority and I learned this the hard way.

I hope by now you are beginning to understand that being a Mumpreneur is not the easy option, it's not an easy way out of 9 to 5 where you will earn loads and do less. It's about planning, time management and making the business you develop work for you, your family and your customers, and believe me this isn't easy!

Checklist – is running a business for you?

- ✓ I have a skill or a qualification that I could turn into a business or have funds to buy a franchise
- ✓ I have good organisational skills
- ✓ I have some funds I can invest in starting my business
- ✓ I can fund my lifestyle until I can draw enough money from my business
- ✓ I can cope with unpredictability
- ✓ I am prepared to ask for advice and get support
- ✓ I can work on my own initiative
- ✓ I am prepared to research my idea and plan
- ✓ I am resilient and can cope with setbacks

I think you need to be able to answer YES to all of these – you must be honest with yourself.

The next chapter is going to deal with the common mistakes made and if you are someone who has already started trading you might find this really useful.

If you are now closing this book and are going to post it on to eBay, then my job is done in that I have made you realise that running a business isn't simple and will require more effort than getting a job.

If you are not closing this book, then we have work to do – so let's get started.

Chapter 2

THE COMMON
MISTAKES
MUMPRENEURS MAKE

No one ever plans to be a Mumpreneur. You don't sit at school with a careers officer and tell them that one day you will start a business to work around your children.

When you have children, life changes dramatically. You find yourself dealing with the stresses and expense of working full time and it can feel very overwhelming. It also means you cannot be there for your children when you would like to as you have to fit around the constraints of an employer. This is when women turn to self-employment as they see this as the answer to these problems.

What are the priorities when starting a business? Deciding in which order to place things can be tricky. This is because there is so much to do and so much information I want to give you. I think this is a book you will dip in and out of – write your notes in it. I have even given you some extra pages at the back for this.

My story (at the back of the book) will tell you all about me but I just want to start by giving you a short summary of what qualifies me to write this book. After all, why should you listen to me?

I became a Mumpreneur in 1998 and since 2011 have also owned a networking company called Mums UnLtd. I also have a successful marketing and events agency which has evolved over time and grown. I have met thousands of Mumpreneurs and in this book I am sharing with you all the things I have seen, heard and personally experienced. So, this is a 'warts and all' account of what it is really like to start a business whilst juggling family life.

Why do some succeed and others fail?

Failure is a word I hate. Mistakes are a learning curve. People who do not make a success of running a business around a family usually have numerous reasons for giving up.

All mistakes are preventable if you get the right advice and support. That's exactly what I am doing in this book by sharing my advice and giving you as many tips and ideas as possible, so you avoid the common pitfalls.

The 12 most common mistakes:

1. Spending too much time faffing around

If you want to start a business, you need to get clued-up and plan. I see too many procrastinating over what to do and how to do it. Absorbed in business names, logos, colours etc. which take up so much time and energy! They get lost before they start!

Start with your idea:

- Research the idea – properly! Is there really a need for your goods/services?

- How big is the potential market? Don't go too niche!

- If it has legs – run with it. If you are unsure – don't!

- You may need to modify your offering once you do the profit check

- The name of a business usually comes to you during this process

- Check no one else is using that name – check with Intellectual Property Office online, this is so important – www.ipo.gov.uk

- Register the name once you have decided on it so you own the trademark ™

- Buy the domain name for the website

2. Not getting the right advice

- Don't just speak to friends and family about your idea, research thoroughly

- Book an appointment with your local enterprise agency, the initial appointment is usually free

- Get a focus group together and talk to your ideal clients

- Go to networking events

- Get a business mentor

3. Not investing in your business

- Yes, you can set it up on a shoestring but even shoestrings cost money

- Do not think you can do this on little or no budget

- What do you need to spend?

  - Domain name and website

  - Business cards and stationery

  - Professional help and training

  - You might need equipment or tools or stock

- The investment is continual – I am still investing in myself and my business 20 years later

4. Not putting in processes and systems from the start

- Post-it Notes – I love them but you can't run your business with them

- To-do lists – fine but you need a way of actively managing your business on the go – as you are going to be on the go with kids

- Bookkeeping – sales automation – the backbone of any successful business

5. Putting the business first

Nope – family first, business second, and make sure you prioritise some time for yourself.

6. Not delegating

So, you are an expert at everything? Err… no you are not. Delegate admin, bookkeeping, maybe marketing, ironing, cleaning, shopping (supermarkets deliver). This is delegation. What you can delegate, do it – don't be a control freak. Don't be obsessive about detail – stop and give yourself a rain check if you are.

7. Not knowing your numbers

- Get an accountant to look through your business plan

- How are you going to make money? Are you going to be able to pay yourself?

- If not, get a job or modify your business plan

- Understand what you need to do to make money – otherwise you don't have a business and you will be a busy fool

8. Not networking

Something you do to gain support, ideas and referrals. You'll really enjoy it when you find the right group.

9. Not listening

- You don't have all the answers. Find people who do and listen to them

- Listen to your customers, listen to the news

- Listening is the skill you need the most and yet people just don't do it

10. Not reviewing and measuring

- What is working and what isn't

- Regular reviews are vital

- Measuring your marketing is essential

11. Not looking at the bigger picture

- Where is the business going, what will it look like in five years?

- Make sure you do some forecasting for 3, 6 and 12 months, then 1, 2, 3 years.

12. Not taking care of yourself and neglecting your family

- You will get sick if you don't look after yourself

- Your family will get annoyed and bored if you don't take care of them

These are the 12 main mistakes I see (and there are more), so make sure you use the advice in this book for prevention, which is far better than cure.

Read all the information in this book. The knowledge in here from myself and other experts will give you a blueprint for success. Plus, all the stories of Mumpreneurs just like you will enable you to understand how they have made their business a success.

Here are some mums sharing their mistakes!

Leigh Farrer, The Salvage Seller, shares why research was vital

I spent a year researching my business and it changed almost monthly. I am glad I spent that time before I had any money as I now have a clearer vision and direction that I want the business to go in. I feel I would have wasted a lot of money had I had it in the research year!

Anna Markovits from Markovits Consulting shares why procrastinating can hold you back

I took quite a long time to 'make the jump' to setting up my own business, and I was worried that because of the economic climate there may not be enough work out there. In hindsight, I wish I had made the jump sooner! The amount of work I am offered allows me to really assess my ability to help each client to achieve their goals and to ensure I am the right fit for them and their organisation, rather than chasing every possible opportunity. As part of my preparations for setting up my business, I had thought about plans if there was not enough work, but I hadn't planned for if there was too much! I should have been more optimistic! My biggest challenge was learning how to run a business and understanding the 'rules' and requirements associated with it.

TAKE ACTION

Get a notebook. Not any old notebook but a really nice one. Use this to make notes about your ideas and record your to-do lists. Although we are all using technology now, I still think having that book to write down your ideas, cross things off and plan is still extremely valuable. But use whatever you feel will work for you. Work with your notebook alongside reading this book. Think about what you have learned from this chapter. Are you already making some of these mistakes? If so put into practice measures to remedy them.

Chapter 3

BRAINSTORM YOUR BUSINESS IDEA

How to profit from your talent or passion and break free from corporate life

The scenario most women face is the dilemma of employed vs self-employed. Have you been left holding the baby and thinking about what to do about your career? You want to do something to keep your brain cells working and to realise your dreams whilst being an amazing mum.

From the outset you must decide what you want to work in terms of hours. You may have to think about how much you need to earn. Everyone has a unique set of circumstances so ignore what everyone else is doing as the important thing is to consider what is right for you and your situation. It boils down to what feels right for you. Use your gut instinct!

If you have decided that you want to think about working for yourself then take your time to consider what type of business you actually want.

TAKE ACTION

Use your notebook and answer these questions

- What skills do you have?

- What interests you?

- Have you always wanted to learn to do something new?

- What are your strengths and what are your weaknesses?

Once you have answered these questions you can consider your options.

The skills you have learned over the years always come in handy at some point! Few schools teach business skills and so most people who start a business don't know where to start. The most important thing is to think about what you are interested in and what you enjoy. If you are working for yourself, you need to love what you do to be motivated to do it.

What are you really passionate about?

Types of business ideas

The Eureka Idea!

This is a business idea which comes to you spontaneously! You could be out walking the dog, in the shower or shopping and you suddenly think of something. Sometimes an idea is born out of an experience you have had. You get that eureka moment and think 'wow, why has nobody thought of this?'!

That is where the research must come in. The business ideas graveyard is full of dead ideas. You must find a business which you can not only breathe life into but keep alive! Is the idea practical, likely to make money and something you would love to do?

The Expert Idea

These ideas come to people who have knowledge and experience of a particular industry. They know they can make their own business work because they have the know-how and contacts to do so. The idea isn't original, but it might be possible to do things differently, better perhaps with new emerging technology. New niches are always a possibility in any industry.

The Business Creation Idea

This is the person who says 'I want to run my own business' but they have no clue what they want to do! They know they cannot work for a company any longer and long for the freedom to create a business they want to do. But at this stage they have absolutely no idea what!

TAKE ACTION

When brainstorming any of these business ideas I think you need to go through a process. Don't skip this – play along even if you are clear as you might find some new ideas come out of this activity.

Get a big piece of paper or use your notebook or laptop.

Answer these questions:

- Is this going to be a fun business – maybe built around a hobby?

- Am I going to be full time or part time?

- Do I want a business which I can grow and employ people but keeping under 15 staff?

- Do I want a business which will require investment and will eventually be a larger scale company?

Write down that goal now – even if at the moment it seems unattainable.

Now you need to generate your ideas and work on them. Here are some more questions to think about when evaluating your ideas:

- Do I need to invest in myself? e.g. training, official qualifications

- What skills do I have? There are so many ideas where you can turn a skill into a business and so many skills you can learn that can become a profit-making business very quickly

- Do some research in your local area – what services are needed?

- What problems can you solve?

- Do people need what you are planning to sell?

- What are your experiences of this industry and who do you know who could help you?

- What is the potential size of the market?

Once you have some options go back to your goal – does this business align with that?

Here are some ideas of businesses that can be started reasonably quickly, depending on your existing knowledge, qualifications and experience, for a reasonable cost, but this list is not exhaustive:

- Virtual assistant

- Bookkeeper

- Accountant

- Marketing consultant

- IFA

- Florist

- Beautician
- Reflexologist
- Massage therapist
- Fitness instructor
- Yoga teacher
- Home tutor
- Website designer
- Cake maker
- Caterer
- PR consultant
- Pets – walking, sitting, minding
- Soft furnishings, dress making and alterations
- Online business – selling goods or services

These are all businesses you can run from home, with small investments and training. These are all low-cost startups and could provide you with a reasonable income. You could also consider buying a franchise – ensure you check carefully and do your research.

Where else can you gain ideas and inspiration?

You could also consider visiting business exhibitions, attending networking events and see what other businesses are offering. This is all part of the research and will give you people to discuss your ideas with. Never be afraid to ask others their opinion on your plans. Many people are scared to do this as they think someone else will steal their idea! So be cautious what you share but I am sure you will find people you can confide in and talk to – your local enterprise agency is a great starting point.

Read books written by great entrepreneurs – this will help you gain confidence and ideas too! Look out for emerging trends and try to see what the ideas of the future could be.

Do what you love doing – otherwise
you will grow to hate it!

Here are a few suggested books:

$100 Startup – Charles Lebeau

The Hard Thing About Hard Things – Ben Horowitz

Become An Idea Machine: Because Ideas Are The Currency of the 21st Century – Claudia Azula Altucher

Business names

Make some time for this, as deciding on a name for a business can be worse than picking the name for your child! But a business name can be changed! Think about what your business does, who you are, where you are based and where you are going to trade. Write a list of words around all these topics.

Why should you dedicate so much time to getting the right name? Firstly, a name should be memorable. This is essential as you build up your brand's reputation. However, a quirky or unique name may not help if it doesn't easily convey what you do.

Equally, a name specific to what you do won't allow much flexibility if you decide to expand or move in a different direction, so consider the future if you go for a name like this.

Finally, your name shouldn't clash with an existing trademark. It can be hard to spend time and resources building up a brand only to lose out because your name is too similar to an existing trademark.

Sometimes when I work with a business I find myself cringing at the name they have – I always ask the background of the name and usually there is some weird convoluted story. But sometimes I get it straight away and I don't even need to ask what someone does as the name conveys that straight away to me. Remember K.I.S.S.

Keep It Simple Stupid!

Don't try and be too clever. Don't try and make up a business name which is too long, too hard to spell or pronounce – you will regret it.

TAKE ACTION

Use your notebook to write down ideas for your business name. Check if other companies are using them. Brainstorm lots of ideas and check for domain name availability and Companies House registration.

Mumpreneur Case Study – An idea to reality ★

Lorry Edwards, Active Creative Ltd.
She has four children plus three stepchildren.
She started her business in 2002.

What does your business do?

Active Creative is the company which delivers Dinky Dancers, Boogaloo Boogie, Motion Commotion, The Performing Arts Club and Fit & Fantastic programmes and classes around the UK. We design and deliver a range of dance, PE, music and action activity programmes to nurseries, children's centres, schools and health clubs nationally. We also promote and deliver musical theatre clubs and dance-based classes for older children, and finally we have a programme called Fit & Fantastic which is an over 50s exercise programme that we deliver in community venues, care homes, residential facilities and health clubs across the country. We also work alongside primary schools to assist them in the delivery of creative movement in the curriculum.

What motivated you to start your business?

I needed to earn a living but also be a stay-at-home mum. So, I set up Dinky Dancers, our creative movement/PE programme for rising two-year-olds, using my experience as a PE teacher, as a way of being able to work flexibly, bring up my children and see if I could contribute to the household income productively.

The hugely positive reaction to the first Dinky Dancers classes rather surprised me, fuelling my motivation and the fire inside me to provide the best programmes and classes I could. I always remember where I started and my financial position. Some people who come to our classes only have a very small amount of disposable money to spend, so therefore, if they choose my classes they will get the best I can possibly deliver. It's something I constantly remind our teaching team of (about 60 staff). Motivation stayed high because the classes were always popular, people wanted to help in the adventure and demand was there, plus I had the opportunity to think about franchising, so I took it and now franchise nationally.

What mistakes did you make when you set up your business?

Trying to do too much all on my own. I would plan work and lessons from 5am-7am before the children woke up, then deliver classes in the day with the children in tow. Then I'd flyer towns and villages, again with the children tagging along. Then from

7pm to 2am I would write lesson plans, policies and training guidance for future class leaders. It was quite tiring, but I knew I had a product which was working. It was so much fun to do, it made money for the family and I was motivated to see how far I could take it! I did everything myself, which was great in the sense that I learned my trade and knew my business inside out. But designing flyers, printing flyers, writing news articles, producing handbooks and writing contracts was not always wise. Being everything to everyone, all the time, probably slowed me down with hindsight. I learned slowly to outsource the areas which are not my gifts and therefore consume time.

How do you juggle family and business?

Determination! My children have been part of this adventure, both the successes and the trials. They have seen how to manage success and failure and how we can do both well. My mum, husband and six of the seven children have or have had part-time roles within the company structure. I won business awards from the Department of Trade and Industry. I was a runner up in 2008 for Hertfordshire Small Business of the Year and then won the award the following year in 2009. My family have seen an idea come from literally nothing to be a success which is still growing. The children have learned flexibility, and they have lived with a strong work ethic.

I have also learned that sometimes it's OK to say no and that I can't do any more today! So, I close the office up, go home, close the curtains and spend proper time with the family. Setting aside mealtimes, breakfast, weekend time has proved vital. I didn't understand that to start with. My teenagers actually need me more now than they did when they were toddlers. I have had to adapt to this and make sure the children have what they need emotionally and usually that's just about giving time. That has meant shoring up the business with a great team who can manage, run and develop things with and, most importantly, without me.

What are your future plans for your business?

Improving and expanding our franchise offering to ensure Active Creative is on offer in as many towns and villages as possible is key to future growth. We are in a phase of restructuring and retraining at head office which is super exciting all round. Supporting our existing franchisees and their teams is our priority, we want to make our franchise support absolutely the best it can be. Making sure each member of our team is doing the best they can for Active Creative's growth and reputation but within their family/personal framework. Giving good, relevant and helpful support as they need it. My biggest success is to know that all my team across the country are working honestly and with integrity. Reputation is everything, so we must model this and make this our absolute focus. We are launching our new Fit & Fantastic programme for the over 50s, which is very exciting. Franchise teams have received training, programmes are ready to go and all the pilot classes we have run have proved super popular

Lorry shares her thoughts on ideas!

All I would add is that if you have an idea, then run with it but do it sensibly. Test the water locally, take advice. Don't throw money into it you don't have – don't tie yourself up in debt. Active Creative cost me £200 to start up, that's all, because I had an idea but not the money. It didn't stop me. I had the drive and worked hard to produce my own materials, used resources I had. Be tenacious, get your business piloted but ask for help along the way. My business owes me nothing, but I owe so much to people around me who were happy to help along the way. Treat people well on the journey, look after your staff and don't run on empty yourself, because that's when you will fall over! My motivation is not necessarily to be the biggest but to offer the best I can.

I grew the business organically, slowly with my family. My mum does our bookkeeping, my husband our franchise finance support, my children all assist at parties and our holiday clubs, as well as bits and pieces of admin in really busy periods. I love that they all get involved! I owe so much to the parents who have come along and still do! I am still excited about every booking we have. I love the fact that we have young people working on our teams who started off as Dinky Dancers aged two. Make sure you work kindly and strongly and keep your family close. It is so possible to do this, but it takes effort and wisdom to make the right choices.

Using someone else's idea – franchises and MLMs

Your business idea brainstorm may lead you to consider buying a franchise or investing into a MLM (multi-level marketing) business and this section will give you some points to consider.

Always get expert advice before buying into any business – ideally a commercial solicitor and your bank.

Buying a franchise, licence or MLM business

Buying a franchise, licence or buying into a multi-level marketing business is an option for some people. So, I am going to explain the difference and what you need to consider.

Anyone trying to sell you a franchise, licence or MLM business will tell you how brilliant it is. They are selling to you and they will rarely give you any of the cons. You may be influenced by someone telling you how great it is for them, they are making loads of money, have a great car etc. but take this all with a pinch of salt as they are telling you because there is money in it for them – your money!

What is a franchise?

A franchise is a complete business model and would typically include business practices, processes, marketing, training and may also include the requirement to purchase materials and products from the franchisor. It should be a complete business in a box.

You need to evaluate whether buying a franchise is right for you by researching thoroughly and answering the following questions:

- You will be told: 'You are buying a proven business system' – but are you? What is this proven 'system'?

- Check with their current franchisees – speak to them. Are they making money? How much support have they had? How difficult has it been to get customers?

- Check what is included – what training will you get, what support, what systems (i.e. website, accounting system, client management systems)?

- What is the cost of the franchise, what royalties will you pay, sometimes called management fees?

- How well known and well respected is the brand? Do you like the name and branding?

- If you have no experience of an industry, buying a franchise may be the route into the industry as they may give you the training and the proven business model making it easier.

What other advice is there to help you decide if a franchise is the right route for you?

I asked franchising expert Krishma Vaghela from Franchise Futures to share her thoughts and top tips.

Krishma said:

I must admit that my nine-year journey in the franchise space has been one fascinating rollercoaster ride. I have seen the good, the bad and the ugly, which truly has given me an insight into franchising. All however worthwhile, as my intention remains to continue in an industry that I believe really does need more of a spotlight shone on it.

I personally think a franchise in some cases can be far less risky than starting up entirely on your own from nothing. A franchise is a proven business model that has been tried and tested by the franchisor and, more often, in multiple locations and in some cases internationally. It is a franchisable concept because it is profitable and clearly the growth potential across the country has been recognised. Banks are far more in favour of lending, especially if the franchise is well established; some can lend up to 70% of the total investment.

You are not only buying into an existing brand name which has been trademarked, you also have the necessary pillars around you to support you in growing your franchise business from the start and towards your upward journey. However, the same cannot be said for when you start your own business.

What do I mean by pillars? The key pillars for a franchisee include marketing support, an existing network of franchisees and a dedicated field-based franchise development or support manager. This, however, is dependent on whether you decide on investing in an 'established' franchise concept or an 'emerging' one. So, let me explain the differences between these.

Emerging franchise: This type of franchise concept is relatively new to the market. The franchisor is probably not established well enough to have all of the necessary resources in place to support a franchisee; however there are many other advantages when you invest in a startup, some of these include:

- A lower investment level

- A wider choice of territories

- Potential to work more closely with the franchisor in developing a stronger business model

Established franchise: The more established a franchise, the more the investment, and the opportunity of you securing the territory you want is far less likely; however there are many positives:

- Greater brand recognition

- More support with marketing

- A dedicated franchise development manager

- A larger franchisee network to engage with and learn from

It is therefore extremely important for you to conduct your research into either option thoroughly.

Below is a quick checklist of what to consider when buying a franchise:

- What are you passionate about?

- What are your key strengths?

- Can you follow someone else's process?

- How much time do you want to commit to the business?

- What is your timescale?

- What location/s are you interested in?

- What type of franchise are you interested in?

  - Managed

  - Bricks and mortar

  - Mobile

  - Home based

- How much do you have to invest up front?

- How much do you realistically need to earn without going into debt?

- Would you consider taking out a loan if required?

Answering these basic questions will get you started on your franchise journey.

Remember, there is a franchise opportunity for everyone and, in most cases, you do not need the industry experience to start a franchise. You have a variety of options but it all starts with you and what is close to your heart; start there and you're bound to succeed!

You can also get advice from **The British Franchise Association (BFA)**. The BFA is a membership organisation with a code of conduct that their members must adhere to. Their website is a major resource and will help guide you to make your decision as to whether buying a franchise is right for you. For example, they have this page with 50 questions you can ask a franchisor:

www.thebfa.org/join-a-franchise/50-questions-to-ask-a-franchisor

You can also speak to your local business adviser at your enterprise agency and your bank.

Both will be able to give you impartial advice.

My advice is get all the facts and listen to your gut.

Here is my story of buying a franchise and the mistakes I made!

Back in 2007 I was trying to find a networking group to join in my local town. This was proving difficult and I came across a company that advertised on their website they were opening a branch of their networking company in my area.

Excited about this, I called them. I spoke to one of the directors who told me that sadly the person who was going to buy the area had just dropped out and during the conversation she asked me if I would be interested in buying the territory. I decided to go along to a meeting they were holding in Essex to see what it was all about. I liked the format, but I wasn't sure about the name of the business and I wasn't sure about them. Something told me they didn't really understand franchising!

They were selling pilot territories for £1,000 so I decided I could make it work. I worked out that the membership fees were sensible, and I would only need five members to make my initial fee back so I felt the risk was minimal. They had two other franchisees at the time. One I spoke to on the phone who seemed very happy, she had been running her groups for a couple of months. The other one had a group around 25 miles from me, so I went along, I really loved the vibe and energy at her meeting and she had 20 members already. So, I decided to put my doubts to one side about the name and the owners and I bought four areas for £4,000.

I launched the first group very successfully, but this was because I put the work in. I found the training they gave me wasn't very useful, the database was useless and the systems they gave me consisted of a plastic box, some chocolates and a spreadsheet! This was 2007 and social media was in its infancy so being found relied heavily on the website and my own word of mouth marketing. Their website was clunky and not appealing.

They quickly sold a lot of territories but had no franchisee recruitment strategy or process; if you had a cheque book you could have a franchise. The business fell apart in September 2009 – not mine, theirs. Franchises were being mis-sold, people lost money and legal action was being taken against them, so they liquidated the business. Mine was solvent. But because they closed the business overnight I was left without a website. No one could book and I had no system for members' information other than what I held personally. I salvaged the situation by renaming the business. I had to invest in a website, new branding, new systems and stationery. I did not lose money but lots of other people did, running into thousands.

I learned the hard way. They were not members of the BFA and my gut feeling told me not to work with them.

To summarise – when buying into any business make sure you do your research (called due diligence) and listen to your gut feeling.

For some people buying a franchise can be a positive experience and a way of getting into an industry you know nothing about. I felt it was important to share this positive story to balance out my negative experience.

Ravneet Bermi, Owner of Puddle Ducks West Herts

Ravneet explains why she started her own business and chose to buy into a franchise.

I was inspired to start my own business to spend more time with my children. I spent over 10 years as a business development manager which I really enjoyed, and I learned a wide range of skills. But after becoming a parent I realised that this career, which included a London commute, was not child friendly. Childcare was expensive, and I worked long hours meaning I had little time to spend with my child.

Whilst continuing to work full time I began to consider the options of running my own business. My weekly highlight was taking my daughter to her baby swimming classes and we always both enjoyed it. I thought this type of business would be really interesting and rewarding and so I decided to qualify in baby and preschool swimming in October 2011.

However, I became pregnant again and this delayed my plans to start the business. After my second child was born I did not want to return to work full time long term and I began to pursue my dream of owning a swimming school.

After extensive research I decided that the franchise route was the best option and was very impressed with Puddle Ducks. They are members of the British Franchise Association, operating since 2001. They had a robust, tried and tested model. Owning a franchise also meant support in such a competitive and legislative business and I felt this would enhance my chances of running a successful and profitable business.

I had researched the area I lived in prior to purchasing the franchise and felt there was a need for more swimming classes.

Getting pool space has proven a challenge but I succeeded in gaining four pools.

Within the first year I exceeded my target of customers by 129%. I set 100 customers as a target for year 1 and ended on 229 customers. My initial marketing plan included using Groupon, something which had not been tried in the swimming class market before. This really helped get the business started. The deal went to 30,000 people, 132 people purchased the offer, 115 redeemed their voucher and 15% of those converted into long-term customers. I have also used Facebook to market the business and entered business awards to raise my profile.

I gained PR in my local newspaper for my charity Pyjama Swim – this gained me some vital PR, raised money for The Children's Trust and helped to gain new customers.

We are almost at the end of year 4 and have 600 customers, 85 classes across seven pools and made a six-figure profit in our year 3 accounts. This was from zero. This demonstrates I have successfully carved out a place in the swimming market using this franchise model.

Licence agreement

A licence gives the licensee the right to use the intellectual property of a business over a defined period in return for a fee. It is seen more as a joint venture and licensees can often be people who have skills the licensor doesn't. It may also mean for example you may have a licence to reproduce something e.g. you could buy a licence to use an image which you can make into promotional merchandise.

Generally, there is no support and you are left to run under the terms of the licence. You would pay a fee, this would be agreed between you and the licence owner and you must abide by the terms of the contract. So, you would not get the same support you would with a franchise.

You must get a solicitor to check any agreement you sign – that goes for a franchise as well as any licence. Never sign anything without doing this.

Multi-level marketing

There is a lot of bad press about this business model. I have been working with people for many years who have bought into various types of MLM models with varying success rates. So, I am going to give you my thoughts on it.

Typically, you will be approached by an existing 'partner' in the business to buy a certain number of products to sell to your network of family, friends or colleagues and they will be encouraged to build a team to do the same. They will be called your 'upline'. Entry level is usually very low, maybe as low as £25, but can be as much as £10,000.

Most will give you all the amazing things that are so positive about the business. You can build an income stream that gets bigger with each person who signs up, you can work flexibly, you can earn unlimited amounts of money, get a car, a holiday, free products, a retirement fund, which all sounds very appealing!

Many of the people who buy into these schemes have used the products themselves and found them beneficial. They are then enticed into thinking this is an easy way to get rich quick. Do not be sucked in – again, do your research as you will still have to work hard to succeed.

Are they a member of the Direct Selling Association? www.dsa.org

They have a code of ethics members must adhere to and there is a lot of information and resources on their website. Their website states:

'Our member companies must provide their independent salespeople with accurate information about products and services, sales and marketing methods and compensation plans.'

If you feel you have not been given accurate information you can contact the DSA and they will deal with the company. You must ask lots of questions and ask to see proof of income; if they do not want to show it to you, walk away. If they are telling you 'I am earning £3,000 a month', say 'show me your bank statements or payment slips from the company' – you want proof.

I have worked with many people on their marketing who have bought into these schemes. I ask them how much they are earning now. It's usually £200-£300 a month. But they bought into the promises of a bigger income in time! Many are not trained properly, given good product training or taught how to run a business! They are set up for failure.

However, I do know people who are successful, but what I have noticed is that they are the ones putting in the serious work. They know they can create compound growth that can lead to hundreds or even thousands of people coming into their business if they work hard to build a team that works hard. If their team is successful, then they will be successful as they will earn an income from the efforts of their team.

The other major factors with an MLM business are that if the entry level is low, you need no experience, and you have no limits geographically; this can be an easier route to setting up a small business.

On the downside some schemes may have minimum orders you need to fulfil each month to keep your status and product discounts, and for some MLM businesses your area may be flooded with people trying to sell the same products or services.

So, do your research, ask lots of questions and never think this will be easy. If you like the products and order regularly, some have preferred customer schemes which is something you might want to consider rather than being a distributor.

My view is only sign up to be a distributor if you want to build a team and are prepared to put in the effort to support and manage them. The only exception to this is when a product may provide you with an additional income stream from your existing clients, e.g. beauty products.

The main things to consider when buying into any business are:

- Could you set up something similar yourself?

- Do you have the finance to do it?

- Do you have the knowledge and skills in that industry?

- If not, can you obtain them another way?

To illustrate my point about buying a franchise I will use the example of a dog-walking business.

You could buy a franchise – costs vary from £2,000 to £16,000. You then have ongoing fees. Some include insurance and a van, cages, use of the brand, training on dealing with dogs and procedures dealing with clients.

I could get trained myself and start my own business. My research told me that I can do some courses on dog walking and dog handling through the British College of Canine Studies from £109: www.britishcollegeofcaninestudies.com. Even if I did five or six courses on their site this would still only be around £1,500.

A website, insurance, and some common sense on business processes would not cost me £1,500. I could lease a van, use a graphic designer to come up with a logo, get a website built. But this of course would take time and money.

Work out the cost to buy a franchise vs the cost of doing it all yourself. Would starting your business your way from scratch and owning 100% of the business be preferable to buying a franchise with royalties to pay? You need to weigh it all up and you need to ask the right questions and do the research to decide.

Summary of Stage One

In the first three chapters of this book we have explored:

- Why do you want to work for yourself?

- The common mistakes Mumpreneurs make

- Brainstorming your business idea

So, before you move on to the nuts and bolts of Stage Two and the actual work involved in building the business, make sure you have thoroughly worked through these chapters and explored your ideas.

My overriding message is the work
you put in to Stage One will
save you time and money later!

STAGE
TWO

Chapter 4

STARTING YOUR BUSINESS - THE ULTIMATE CHECKLIST

Once you have decided what you are going to do and have taken the relevant training if required, the next step is to actually start to trade.

Some of this chapter will apply to you if you are purchasing a franchise, licence or MLM business so make sure you read this all very carefully and work out your action list.

There are a number of things you need to do to get this business going. I have put together this list for you to work through and set yourself some goals, so you don't procrastinate! I meet so many people who tell me that it took years to get the business going because they really didn't know what they should do and in what order!

1. Business Plan

Even if you do not want finance for your business it is still vital to write a business plan so you have a clear direction on your business. Also it can help you to face questions and issues you might otherwise ignore.

The business plan will help you to plan clear goals, be proactive not reactive, and make better business decisions. It will also help you gain clarity on your numbers.

The following list is an idea of what to include and questions to ask yourself when preparing this information.

1. Summary

Usually best to do this last! Build a summary about all the areas you have talked about. Fill around half of an A4 page. Imagine someone had a couple of minutes to read all about your business and you wanted to entice them to read more.

2. Business overview

Introduction – Include who you are and what you do. Assume your reader knows nothing about you or your business.

Current position – Are you trading, if so for how long? Company set-up e.g limited company/sole trader/partnership.

Competitive advantage – What makes you the best? Why will you succeed in your market?

Growth plan – What are the plans to grow the business? Think about three to five years.

3. Business strategy

Tactics – What tactics will you use to grow your business?

Strategic issues – What internal and external threats do you face? What changes might there be in your industry or with your customer base?

Core values – What are the core values of your business?

4. Marketing

SWOT and critical success factors – Strengths/Weaknesses/Opportunties and Threats.

Market research – What research have you completed about your market and industry? Who are your competitors? Who are your customers?

Distribution channels – How will you distribute your products/services?

Strategic alliances – Who can you partner with?

E-commerce and technology – Do you have a website? What other means of technology do you use to promote your business online or manage your business?

Tactical promotion plan – Promotions/discounts.

Marketing budget – How much are you spending on your marketing annually and how will this increase as the business grows? How much does each customer cost to aquire?

Credibility and risk reduction – How will your credibility be measured? What steps have you taken to reduce risk?

5. Team and management structure

Skills, experience, training and retention – Information on the team.

Advisers – Who else is involved in your business?

Management systems – Think about staff handbook/process manuals/HR/health and safety/payroll.

6. Financial budgets and forecasts - best to show on a spreadsheet

Profit and loss account – A profit and loss account does just what it says on the tin: it tells you what profit or loss you will make *over a certain period of time* – i.e. from one date to another. It is sometimes also called an income and expenditure statement. Your sales/ income, less what it actually costs you to make those sales, will give you your gross profit. You will then deduct all other expenditure, classed as indirect costs – things like rent, rates, electricity costs etc., and that will then give you your net profit (or loss). The net profit figure is the important one, not the gross profit, as even if you are making a gross profit, you may be making a loss when all other costs have been deducted.

Cash flow forecast – A cash flow forecast predicts the expected cash in and out of the business over a certain future period of time – usually covering a 12-month period, month by month. The cash flowing into the bank account, less the cash expected to go out of the bank account will give you the *net cash flow*, and of course you want this to be a positive figure. This figure should represent the bank balance in each of those periods. This is crucial when you are starting up – many profitable companies have failed because they didn't manage their cash flow properly. If you don't know how to do a cash flow statement, get help and advice from an accountant.

Balance sheet statement – The balance sheet statement is a snapshot of the business at a specific point in time (as opposed to over a period of time like a profit and loss account and a cash flow forecast). A balance sheet statement, in summary, shows four categories:

- Fixed assets – these will be the things the business owns that you could physically touch, such as vehicles, equipment etc.

- Current assets – these are assets that you cannot touch, so things like money owed to you from customers (called debtors), stock, and cash in the bank

- Long-term liabilities – these are exactly what the name suggests – things you owe that do not need to be paid back in the short term, such as loans

- Current liabilities – these are short-term liabilities (debt) – anything you owe that will need repaying in the short term e.g. VAT, overdraft and PAYE

Fixed assets + current assets = total assets
Less
Long term liabilities + current liabilities

Gives you your net assets – the value of your company

This is 'balanced' (hence the name balance sheet) with the way you have financed the business called:

Capital and reserves – this will be any shareholder investment, and any retained profits (called reserves). This is a cumulative record of all your company's profits that have not yet been distributed either as dividends or invested back in the business.

Capital investment – the amount of money you need to set up.

Capital expenditure – other large investments you make in the business once it's up and running.

Break-even point – this is the point where you are not making any losses or profits – the point where your income equals your expenditure. After this point, you will start making a profit. On a profit and loss account, this is where your net profit/loss = zero.

7. Business insurance – my advice is talk this through with an insurance broker

You will need to consider the risks for the type of business you have and what you need cover for. So, for example, if you are working with the general public you may need public liability or professional indemnity insurance. If you have stock or equipment that might get stolen or damaged then you might want to insure that. If you have employees you will need employer's liability insurance. Make sure you discuss this with an expert who can help you decide what you need.

For business plan templates:

https://www.gov.uk/write-business-plan
http://www.bplans.co.uk/sample_business_plans.cfm
www.businesslink.gov.uk/...Business.../Business_Plan_Template_v8.4.do

Your bank/accountant may also have a template.

TAKE ACTION

Download a template and work through all the areas in the plan. You can work on this over a period of time. Completing a plan before you get started then updating as you go will ensure you are on track and focused.

---

2. Your message

Your message is a clear, well thought-out mission statement. Before you go any further, do this piece of work. Do not order any stationery or confirm your business name until you have done this! This underpins all that the business offers and who your target market is.

1. You must work out exactly who you can help and what they need! What problem are you solving? What you are bringing to their life? Often, I find people think they know, but they don't do their research. This leads to lots of time and effort wasted and confusion with the overall brand and marketing message.

2. Once you have worked out your ideal client then you need to brainstorm ideas of branding and messages that would appeal to them. You need your target clients to take notice of you. They will only do this if your message resonates with them.

3. Look at competitors and businesses you admire.

4. Your message must convey and prove your expertise and passion.

5. Think about case studies and stories, studies and statistics, myth busting and comparisons. Google hosts a wealth of knowledge on almost anything.

6. Think about how you are going to bond with your ideal client and compel them to take action. You want a message and a brand which will open their mind up to working with you or buying your products or service. Illustrate why they should choose you: you are the best option because…

7. You need to be clear on what you offer. Make sure your business will get the desired results – the heart of your business is your customer.

8. When thinking about your message don't underpin it all with 'We offer the best service' or 'We are the best priced in the area'. Don't overuse the word 'we', slate competitors or use 'great service' as part of your message. Great service should be standard with any business.

If you find this difficult, work with a marketing or branding consultant to help you.

It is so important to be very clear on your message and who you are targeting.

3. Your accounts

Contact HMRC (Tax Office) and advise them you are becoming self-employed.

You'll need to:

• Keep records of your business's sales and expenses

• Send a self-assessment tax return every year

- Pay Income Tax on your profits and Class 2 and Class 4 National Insurance; use HMRC's calculator to help you budget for this

- Decide on a business name – check this carefully and make sure you are not infringing on anyone else's copyright

As a sole trader or ordinary business partnership you don't have to register with Companies House but you still need to follow the rules for choosing a business name. Your name can't be the same as another registered company's name; search the Companies House register to see if a name has been taken.

Your registered company or LLP name can't be similar to another registered name. Your business name also can't:

- Contain a 'sensitive' word or expression unless you get permission

- Suggest a connection with government or local authorities

- Be offensive

Your name must be unique – it can't be the 'same as' or 'too like' an existing name.

- **Decide on the set up – sole trader, partnership or limited company**

I strongly advise you to get expert advice on this. Speak to an accountant or business adviser and HMRC are very helpful.

- **VAT registration**

You must register for VAT if your annual turnover is over £85,000 or if you think it will be (correct as of 2018). You can register voluntarily if it suits your business, for example if you sell to other VAT-registered businesses and want to reclaim the VAT. Again, check with your accountant.

It is also advisable to set up a bank account in your business name; it's much easier to keep your personal and business records separate and looks more professional. Most banks offer free business banking for a limited period. Shop around for the best rates.

4. Buy your website domain name

Think carefully about this. Choosing a domain name for your website is vital to produce great results that will drive traffic to your web page. Don't choose anything too long or anything too like anyone else. Choosing a domain name that is the same as or quite similar to another well-known trademark may lead to legal action. And if it's a big brand, you might face a big penalty or get sued. So, it's always recommended to check for existing trademarks before choosing a domain name. Also check if you can use the domain name on social media.

The wrong domain selection can get you into trouble and cause you much difficulty later on. Most importantly, a good domain name selection may increase your opportunities for getting better Search Engine Results Page (SERP) rankings. Taking time to research and learn the history of your domain will be imperative to your long-term success.

Make sure you do a background check. If you are preparing to buy a domain name you really need to check domain names for a history of problems before you risk your online business future. Check the Whois database www.whois.com. This provides basic information about the owner of the domain and where it is hosted. If the domain name isn't currently registered, you can purchase it.

Sometimes a domain may have been used before and could be blacklisted by Google. You can check online at one of these sites. Tools to check if a domain is banned by Google or google AdSense:

- bannedcheck.com

- isbanned.com

- iWebTool

5. Get a logo created

What to consider:

- What do your competitors use and think how you want to differentiate from other businesses in a similar industry to you.

- Think about your message and what you are trying to communicate. Make sure you have completed the work on your message, so you can work out who you are targeting.

- A logo should be functional – it should work well on a business card, flyer, banner stand, promotional items and consider what else you will use it for. It should read well in colour and black and white.

- Make sure it's distinctive and clear and the best logos are simple and sleek in design.

- Never use Clip Art.

- Consider the colours carefully – one that has four or five colours may look lovely but will be expensive to print on promotional items. Go with one or two, maximum three.

- Get someone to design it for you but do some research and maybe some sketches first.

- Your logo is the foundation on which the business is built so make sure it will last and you love it.

- Once it's all designed, protect it. You can register it with Intellectual Property Office.

6. Set up a website

Why do you need a website?

In my view a website is essential as you need to reach potential customers through the search engines, social media and a place for existing customers to buy products or services.

Most people search for what they want online, and if you are not there you will miss valuable business. If you don't have an online presence, it's more than likely that a potential customer will pick a competitor that does.

Building your website

Choose a simple domain name, nothing too long or complicated and make sure it makes sense! Register it with a domain service such as Fasthosts or 123-reg.co.uk

When it comes to designing and building a business website, you have three options:

1. If you have some great technical skills you could build it yourself!

2. You can buy a DIY template builder.

   Low-cost DIY websites usually include web building, hosting and a domain name, and are largely made up from simple templates which you customise yourself. I won't name any as the market changes but the prices are generally very low because you have to pay for the extras that actually make the website work well – e.g. search engine optimisation and features such as additional storage and bandwidth. Plus, on a free or low-cost platform site your customers might be subjected to advertisements.

I have worked with a lot of businesses over the years that have started on these platforms. They are restricted by the themes provided and not getting found on Google.

3. You can go to a web design agency and get them to do it for you.

Many companies have lowered their fees over the years as the market has become more competitive, so you can find companies offering competitive prices for website design. If you have anything complicated and want an e-commerce store for example then it is worth getting quotes from companies who know this market well and can provide you with a website which performs well. Always get a site you can update yourself.

7. Get some business stationery

Most businesses start with business cards. Here are my top business card tips:

- Don't go for black backgrounds

- Make sure people can write on it, so no metal or shiny card

- Make sure it has all your contact information including social media

- Make it dual purpose so you could use it for appointments or have a special offer on it

You might need to consider leaflets, brochures, banner stands, appointment cards. It does depend on your business. Make sure you have clear concise literature that looks professional.

8. Set up your social media platforms

Consider carefully what is needed – you should pick a platform you think your customers are using. You will also need to consider what training you might need to use these platforms effectively.

Social media is part of your marketing plan and should not be the only marketing channel you use to market your business. Here are a few ideas to get you started. There is more information on this in Chapter 7 which covers all aspects of marketing.

- Facebook – set up a business page and for this you will need a personal profile. Make sure your company name is available and do not use a personal profile as a business. Use photos and videos to illustrate your business

- You could consider a Facebook group to attract your ideal clients

- Instagram is now also popular particularly with a younger audience

- Do not set up Twitter unless you are going to use it

- LinkedIn is a must as that helps with Search Engine Optimisation

- A Google account is vital as you will need that to connect to your website, plus you can then create a places listing

9. More research

Hopefully you did quite a lot of research in Stage One. However, once you have got some initial research done and know your idea is a viable one, you should do some more research at the point where you have ideas for your logo, business name and services you are going to offer. Listen to this feedback. You should find this really useful in shaping your pricing, your message and branding. Make sure you speak to your target market. For example, there is no point in talking to people about a premium product or service if they are on a low income!

Once you have your website live, ask people to do some usability testing. This means asking for views and opinions on how your website works for a potential customer. How easy is it for people to find the information they need? How easy is it to purchase an item? Ask someone to do a test purchase for you. Gather the feedback and tweak the site where needed.

Why not set up a market research group? Invite 10 people along and ask them lots of questions about your products and services. You may need to do a few of these, getting up to 50 people's opinions could save you time and money later.

10. Pricing

Call other companies that are doing something like you. Find out what they charge – pretend to be a prospect, don't hide behind emails, call them! If you can't find any company doing the same as you, think about similar industries and think about the market you will be offering the services to. What do you think your target customers would be prepared to pay? This is where speaking to family and friends can help.

You could set up a survey online. Survey Monkey (online service) is free for short surveys. Send it round on email and Facebook asking for people's views on pricing. If you are still unsure, go lower than you think as it's always easier to put your price up than lower it and risk annoying customers who paid more for the goods and services. Or price higher and have introductory offers which give discounts.

Pricing is always a sensitive subject with female business owners. Charging what you are worth can be tricky and lots of startups lack confidence in this area. As I have grown in experience and gained more qualifications, I have felt justified to increase my pricing. Don't undercut the competition – charge the market rate for your goods or services.

If you need help and advice, talk to a business coach or your local enterprise agency who generally are happy to advise.

11. Write your marketing plan

This needs to be specific and again is essential.

Look at promotions to get your first customers on board. This will be built into your marketing plan, but I just thought I would mention it here to get your creative juices going. We have covered everything you need to know in Chapter 7.

12. Systems and processes

How will you process customer orders? Keep track of your clients? You need a system for keeping track of prospects and for managing your accounts online. By considering these early you will save time and money later. See Chapter 9 for more details.

Mumpreneur Case Study – Setting up an accountancy practice ★

Lara Apoola, HarmonyBooks, has two children aged 16 and 11.

I was brought up in Nigeria from the age of eight so there was a massive focus on being well educated. It was expected that you would go to university. I aspired from an early age to have my own business and when I told my parents they were adamant that a degree was vital. We returned to England and I went to Thames Valley University and got a degree in Accounting and Finance. Once I graduated I got my first job as an accounts assistant and then over the years worked for a variety of companies and worked my way up to a senior accountant role.

I had my first child in 2002 and I went back to work when she was four months old. I didn't have any issues with juggling work and my daughter as I had support from my mum and I had found a good nursery, which I finalised while I was pregnant. In my industry at that time there were lots of women in the same situation. I had no choice but to continue to work full time as we just couldn't afford for me to give up; with a high mortgage and bills, staying at home wasn't an option.

I had my second child in 2008 and returned to work again; I did take the full maternity leave which I didn't do the first time. Having two children was harder when I was working full time. By now my elder daughter was at school. This meant getting up very early, coping with traffic jams and getting two children ready could be stressful. My employer didn't understand about the problems of combining working with motherhood. She didn't like me to take time off to go to school plays, sports days and ballet recitals even though I said I would make up the time. This made me very upset and I felt I just couldn't continue working for an employer. I had been suffering with stress for so long, I had constant migraines, and this was due to the work situation.

I made the decision to leave. It was near Christmas and I took a couple of months off to decide what I was going to do. I was going to look for another job but when I discussed it with a friend I used to work with, he suggested I could work for myself.

He pointed out I had literally turned around the last business I worked for and set up systems for them and really got the business on the right track. He made me think that if I could do that for someone else I could definitely do it for myself.

So, I decided to set up HarmonyBooks and aimed my business at small business owners who needed bookkeeping and accountancy services such as tax and VAT returns. The 10 years I worked as a practice accountant gave me invaluable experience so my company was set up to fulfil the accounting and bookkeeping needs of clients ranging from sole traders to limited companies – experience which has inspired me to start a bookkeeping company with a different kind of ethos.

I recognised that some SMEs required a little more time and nurturing through the maze of accounting and bookkeeping, whilst some companies require only minimal help; some may prefer their bookkeeper on site and some may prefer to have their bookkeeping managed externally. Therefore, the ethos of the business is to provide a great quality bookkeeping service, just as often as each individual client needs, at a location to suit them.

Starting a business was scary as I didn't have any money to invest in the business or any money to support myself. I hated asking my husband for money and at times in the first couple of years it was a strain on our finances, but he was supportive of me.

It took almost two years to make a profit and there were times I was thinking I should go back to work as I would earn more. But we made cutbacks and sacrificed having two cars, we paid school fees by instalments, as our children were in private school, and had to cut back on holidays. I carried on with the business as I wanted to be there for the children.

If I worked from 9 to 5 I knew I wouldn't see them anywhere near as much. My younger daughter needed help with homework and support that I felt only I could give. My elder daughter was very independent but the younger one less so. I also felt less pressure as I could sit through a school play and not be clock watching and rushing back to work. My younger daughter did more hobbies as I had more time. When I worked they couldn't do activities as there was no one to take them. The welfare and happiness of my children and myself came before having more money. I was so much more relaxed and felt so much better working for myself even though I wasn't earning as much as I would have done had I had a job.

I found business networking really valuable. It helped build my confidence and I did get business from it plus lots of advice and support. I learned a lot from others about running my business and this really helped. I found you can build really good relationships and I was happy to help others with tax advice if they needed it.

My business is something I can do around my children and if I was working in a practice as an employee I wouldn't have as much flexibility. Even though my girls are now 16 and 11, I have no plans to return to full-time employment and intend to stay self-employed.

As a bookkeeper and accountant my advice is to keep good records, set up systems early on. You don't need to spend a fortune on software for your accounts, just keep your receipts in a folder. See where your business goes before spending money on software as you may not need it. If you are a business with a lot of transactions and are VAT registered I would recommend getting a bookkeeper early on and getting some tax advice.

TAKE ACTION

Chapter 4 has a lot of actions! You need to work through the 12 steps meticulously. You will find additional help in this book on each part of these steps. Break down the tasks into a to-do list in your notebook. Set yourself goals when you will complete each step.

Chapter 5

FUNDING

Funding is a question that comes up a lot with the Mumpreneurs I work with. Usually it's because they are broke! Most have struggled through maternity leave and now have little ones to feed and clothe. They want to earn an income but do not have the money to start a business.

You can start a basic business for very little and work at reinvesting some of the profits into your business. Many people will fund their startups through their own savings, but if you need expensive equipment, premises or anything else that is going to require thousands of pounds you may need to consider other forms of funding.

Startup funding is not easy to obtain!

My advice is spend time doing some research.

Grants may be available in your area; startup loans change constantly so this chapter will discuss the different types of funding, so you can understand all those terms which seem very confusing. There is also a list of some websites to check out the latest information.

Work out your startup costs

When you start up your business you will need to ensure you know what it is going to cost you. That is part of your business plan, so spend some time thinking about this and planning your costings. You should have done this in previous chapters, but if you have gone straight to this section go back to the earlier chapters in the book.

How much can you raise?

Do you have some savings, equity in your property, items you can sell?

Check out these websites

For startups, the first place to check is this website. This is a listing of grants and loans which might be available to you. This website also includes details of free support in your area.

http://startups.co.uk/how-to-find-the-right-route-to-funding/

https://www.gov.uk/business-finance-support

You may also find grants and bursaries for specific sectors.

Talk with your bank – some have small business advisers.

You can also try https://www.startuploans.co.uk/

You may also be at the point where your business is established, it is making a profit and you need funds to grow further. This may be to hire staff, move to larger premises or invest in equipment and you need the additional cash injection to scale the business. I am not going to discuss business growth in this book beyond getting started and the first year or two. Once you have reached this point you need more advice and you can get this from a number of different sources.

There are people and companies that invest in startups – Dragons' Den style!

Angel investors

Angel investors tend to be high-profile business leaders who choose to invest either the full amount of money you need, or a significant amount, into your business. So, you get not only the financial support but the personal backing from someone already well established in business who can provide access to unique contacts to help your company succeed.

It's important to outline the expectations from the start before entering into any funding agreements. Lay down rules and a framework. Only work with an angel investor that shares your goals for the business and decide on the duration of the agreement.

Investor funding can be an incredibly powerful source of funding for new businesses. It means that the business has been funded solely on the potential of your business idea and shows a clear belief that your business will succeed.

Find more information here: www.ukbusinessangelsassociation. org.uk

Crowdfunding

Crowdfunding is another way of raising finance. Basically, you post your business idea online, in keeping with their rules of course, and you can reach a large number of people who will invest small amounts in your business, often for products or a small share of your profits. Social media plays a massive role in the success of these projects and you really have to get behind promoting it.

Check out this website for more information: www.ukcfa.org.uk

There are different types of crowdfunding.

Reward-based crowdfunding

This method of raising finance has become very popular over recent years for gaining investment, great for developing an awareness of your brand.

If you have a product-based business, crowdfunding rewards can work really well to gain not only finance but new customers and brand awareness. Investors pledge money in return for being sent a product or a discount on a future purchase. It might be a special one-off item or part of your new product line. You can start the level of funding at just £5 up to thousands and the biggest advantage is the awareness you are building for your new business. These people will become your customers of the future!

Kickstarter is a crowdfunding platform for people in the arts. They typically help artists, musicians, filmmakers, designers, and other creators find the resources and support they need to make their ideas a reality. To date, tens of thousands of creative projects – big and small – have come to life with the support of the Kickstarter community. Again, they have created a great buzz around their project!

Crowd Cube is one of the most popular and successful crowdfunding sites. They have made investing accessible, affordable and rewarding by enabling everyday investors to invest alongside professionals and venture capital firms in startups, early and growth stage businesses.

Business competitions

There are business competitions out there – you just have to find them. Often these come with prize money for your new business or money you can use to grow and develop. There is also the added bonus of gaining attention and much needed press. You will also get to meet with the sponsors and possibly the odd business celebrity or two! As any list I would write on this would quickly go out of date, this website is a good resource. You can also do a Google Search 'Business Competitions':

http://entrepreneurhandbook.co.uk/competitions-award/

Many local councils offer a Dragons' Den type competition with awards of around £1,000 so worth checking. If you are starting a green business or technology business there are competitions, grants and funding so do check carefully. Your local enterprise agency should be able to advise you of any grants or funding in your area so make sure you check with them.

Taking on a business partner

Some people take on a business partner to further develop their business idea and this partner puts in some funding in exchange for equity. Do not do this without really thinking it through. I have worked with a lot of people who have had a drunken night with a friend and decided they should start a business! In most cases this ends in tears.

Going into business with friends, family, ex-work colleagues or business associates isn't something you should do without fully considering the aspects from all sides and taking legal advice! For any partnership to work the boundaries must be clear, there must be a contract drawn up and the equity you each own must be fair.

The boundaries revolve around deciding at the outset who does what and when. How will the day to day running of the business work? Look at the skill sets you both have. The best partnerships are those where each partner has different skill sets but they share values and goals.

So, for example, if you are forward thinking and want to invest in the latest gadgets and technology for your business and your partner doesn't, you will quickly get frustrated. You need to sit down and brainstorm together for several days the business idea and how the partnership may work before you spend any money.

If you work with someone on the idea for a couple of weeks, day in day out, you will start to get a feel if you could work with this person. As I have said in other areas in this book – trust your gut.

Never do work for anyone for free on the promise of getting a share of the business and never expect that of anyone.

Make sure you get proper contracts drawn up by a solicitor as this could save you thousands in the future.

Asset finance

If you need a van, company car or large equipment (fridges are a good example), asset finance allows you to apply for a loan against those items which are essential to your business. An asset finance loan means that your company can lease the necessary equipment during the loan and, depending on the loan terms, you may be able to take ownership of the equipment outright at the end of the loan agreement. You must be confident that you will be able to cover the costs over the period of the loan so make sure you have done plenty of number crunching!

TAKE ACTION

Work out your costs, income projections and how much money you will need. Make sure you are obtaining funding for essential items to get the business started. It is nice to have a shiny new Mac but is this a necessity? Whatever you decide, make sure you research and consider it carefully.

Here are some more websites you might find useful:

http://entrepreneurhandbook.co.uk/grants-loans/ – this website has a list of grants and loans

http:// www.startuploans.co.uk – government backed with free business support

http:// www.Fundinglondon.co.uk – they look to invest in high-growth tech, science and digital startups in London http://www.connectlondon.org – funding, mentoring and academic support

http://www.j4bgrants.org.uk – a directory of grants and funding support

http://www.fredericksfoundation.org – loans for startups refused elsewhere London wide

http://www.princes-trust.org.uk – funding for training and business startup with support and mentoring for people aged 18-30

Mumpreneur Case Study – How crowdfunding worked for me ★

Gemma Whates, All By Mama, shares her story of crowdfunding. She is 35 and has two children.

All By Mama is a marketplace and community for businesses that are run by mums. We offer our Mamas a place to sell their products, network together and receive advice and support to help grow their businesses.

The business launched in November 2014, although planning started about nine months prior as we researched and developed the brand and website. We are a different business today from the business we were at launch, we've learned as we've grown.

Why did you crowdfund?

We have a big vision: to be the world's best marketplace for parent-run businesses. We believed investment would help accelerate our growth and allow us to reach a wider market, raising awareness of the brand and what we can offer our customers and sellers. It would also help us to develop some of the resources we would like to offer sellers and customers. Crowdfunding felt right for us for the stage we are at with our business and we wanted to offer our customers an opportunity to share in our business and our future success.

How did you do it?

With a lot of hard work! The entire process took around six months and isn't to be underestimated. From the preparation (which is great as it really gets your business in shape if it isn't already) to the actual campaign which was a full-time job for the five weeks that it ran and then the close of the campaign and the leads that followed. We worked with a fantastic adviser who helped us through the process. It was a lot of work to mobilise our 'crowd' before we could engage with potential investors and we learned so much during the process. We brought some great people into the business and it's opened lots of doors.

Who did you use?

Crowdcube, an equity crowdfunding platform.

How much did you raise?

£76,000.

Benefits?

It is a great way to raise finance for an early stage business, generates awareness for the brand and obviously provides much needed capital. You also create a group of brand ambassadors who want your brand to succeed and who might be interested in offering their experience.

Any issues?

It can be difficult to keep the day to day business running if you are a small team, as you will have questions to answer from potential investors every day. You have limited time to make the campaign a success. But during that period your workload will double, hard to manage when you're running a small business.

Anything else you feel would be relevant to someone crowdfunding for the first time?

Make sure you do as much preparation work as possible, planning how you will generate interest. Don't believe that just putting the campaign live will be enough, you need to drive it. Generate some interest from your own crowd before you begin to help build momentum, ensure your finances and projections have been well thought through and put a reasonable valuation against your business that works for your future plans and for anyone investing. Lastly, if you can, get some additional help to run the business while you focus on the campaign.

Chapter 6

MANAGING YOUR
BUSINESS FINANCES

I am lucky to know so many awesome experts and Hannah Miller is one of them. I asked her to share her best tips on managing your accounts and running your business, so you know you are making money!

When you set up your business you need to:

- Prepare a business plan and include projections for the first two to three years

- Arrange a meeting with your bank to obtain free information and advice

- Open a business bank account so that business transactions are easy to track and are kept separate from personal expenditure

- Set up direct debits and use your business credit card as much as possible

- Set up an invoice template and a credit control system to track invoices paid and keep receipts for purchases

- Determine how you will maintain accurate business records; there are many bookkeeping software packages available to assist including free packages

- Putting robust systems in place from day 1 when you have more time will benefit the business in the long term

Ongoing tasks

- Review the bank account on a regular basis and perform a bank reconciliation at least monthly

- Track the business income and expenditure and compare to the forecast in your business plan

- Calculate profits to measure the bottom line

- Calculate an estimate of the tax due and put the money aside, for example in a separate bank account

- Monitor cash flow

- Set up a system for keeping receipts

Business structure

- The business could be structured in different ways, for example, a sole trader, a partnership or a limited company.

- Seek professional advice at an early stage to ensure the optimal business structure for your business.

- Sole trader: a sole trader is a self-employed person trading in their own name. The business is not a separate legal entity and you can take drawings out of the business at any time. The taxable profits are included on the individual's personal tax return.

- Partnership: a partnership may be automatically established if two or more people are in business together. A partnership agreement should be put in place setting out the capital and profit split between the partners. The partners include their profit share on their own tax returns and pay Income Tax and National Insurance contributions. There is no protection and the partners are jointly and severally liable for any debts.

- Limited company: a limited company is a separate legal entity. Directors run the business and shareholders own the business. It is possible to set up a business with only one director/shareholder and many small businesses are set up as limited companies.

- Benefits

  - Protection of limited liability.

  - Certain tax savings if structured properly. The main tax saving is National Insurance since a director/shareholder usually takes a low salary and extracts profits as dividends. There is no National Insurance on dividends but dividends are now taxed at higher rates, so the savings have reduced.

  - Flexibility of timing of profit extraction. You can determine when to take the money out the company if you have different levels of taxable income in different tax years or wish to leave the profits in the company (to achieve lower Capital Gains Tax rates on exit).

  - Reduced Corporation Tax rates since the tax rate is falling from 20% to 17% by April 2020.

  - Perception since a limited company may appear more attractive to customers.

- Drawbacks

  - The costs of running a limited company are higher due to paying an accountant for the statutory filing at Companies House in addition to running a payroll scheme and filing company and personal tax returns.

  - The day to day operation is more complex together with taking money out of the company since the company is a separate legal entity.

  - It is more difficult to close down a limited company.

  - Certain information is held on the public record at Companies House.

Dealing with HMRC

- A sole trader should register as self-employed with HMRC as soon as the business starts: https://www.gov.uk/log-in-file-self-assessment-tax-return/register-if-youre-self-employed

- The deadline for registering with HMRC for a self-assessment tax return is 5 October following the end of the tax year which runs from 6 April to 5 April.

- Registering online at the outset should ensure that registration has been made for both Income Tax (self-assessment) and National Insurance since they are separate offices and will avoid missing the above deadline. Alternatively register by phone by calling both offices.

- Self-employed [Class 2] National Insurance is £2.80* a week if your profits exceed £5,965 per annum and is payable together with Income Tax on 31 January following the end of the tax year. Class 4 National Insurance is payable at 9% on profits between the limits £8,060 and £43,000 and at 2% on profits over £43,000* and is payable with Income Tax.

- There may be benefits in paying voluntary Class 2 National Insurance, for example in the first year when profits are low to obtain a year's National Insurance credit for state pension purposes. If you are claiming child benefit, then you automatically receive a credit until the child is 12.

- A partnership should also be registered with HMRC, so it has its own tax reference.

- A limited company has its own tax reference and accounting date depending on the date of incorporation and pays Corporation Tax.

- A director/shareholder of a limited company may need to register for self-assessment to pay additional Income Tax.

- Income Tax is payable on 31 January following the end of the tax year. If Income Tax and Class 4 National Insurance on your last tax bill exceed £1,000, then payments on account are required. Payments on account are 50% of the prior year tax liability payable on 31 January in the tax year and 31 July after the end of the tax year. Any balance is payable when the tax return is filed on 31 January following the end of the tax year.

Setting up a limited company

- There are many formation agents who will set up limited companies for a small fee or this can be readily done online at Companies House.

- An accountant can also set up a limited company and will be needed to file the statutory accounts and tax return.

VAT

You must register for VAT if your turnover is over £85,000 in any 12 month period or if you think it will be in the next 30 days (correct as of 2018). You can register voluntarily if it suits your business, for example if you sell to other VAT-registered businesses and want to reclaim the VAT. Again, check with your accountant.

- You would then charge VAT at 20%* on your invoices and offset VAT paid on your purchases.

- VAT returns and payments are generally made quarterly and there are certain schemes available which may benefit the business.

- There may be benefits of voluntarily registering for VAT even if the business's profits do not exceed £85,000, particularly if your customers are VAT registered and can reclaim the VAT.

This enables your business to reclaim VAT on purchases.

- Keep good business records and VAT receipts for all purchases.

Expenses

- Ensure that business expenses are paid through the business bank account to ensure that all business expenses are included.

- Establish which expenses are allowable for tax purposes. For example client entertaining is not allowable: https://www.gov.uk/expenses-if-youre-self-employed

- Keep track of pre-trading expenditure before the business starts.

- Capital expenditure may be eligible for capital allowances.

- Keep track of business mileage and reclaim this expense from the business, although ordinary commuting may not be allowable. There are different rules for the tax treatment of travel expenses depending on the business structure.

- A sole trader can use simplified expenses, for example to claim use of a home office: https://www.gov.uk/simpler-income-tax-simplified-expenses/overview

It is also advisable to set up a bank account in your business name; it's much easier to keep your personal and business records separate and looks more professional. Most banks offer free business banking for a limited period. Shop around for the best rates.

Software

- There is plenty of bookkeeping software including free software:
https://www.gov.uk/expenses-if-youre-self-employed

- Choose a software package which suits your business, for example certain software may benefit a cash business.

- Many software packages will pull the bank transactions from your bank automatically.

- There are software packages which automatically book the expense and VAT by reading scanned bills.

- You do not need to be a bookkeeper to use this software but ensure the records are kept up to date and checked.

- Alternatively, records can be maintained in Excel. Create a sales ledger, a purchase ledger and cashbook and regularly reconcile the bank account.

Making tax digital

- HMRC has introduced proposals for taxpayers to file records digitally on a quarterly basis so HMRC can calculate tax liabilities in real time.

- It is proposed for the new rules to apply to non VAT registered sole traders from April 2018, VAT registered sole traders from April 2019 and limited companies from April 2020. If income exceeds £10,000 per annum then quarterly reporting is required, although this threshold may change. The due dates for Income Tax are currently unchanged.

- HMRC have advised that free software will be available, and spreadsheets can be used provided the data can be submitted through software.

- While the final proposals are not known at time of publication, any new business should bear the changes in mind when determining how to maintain their records.

Getting help

- Engaging an accountant at the outset is beneficial to discuss the optimal business structure, allowable expenses and a suitable bookkeeping package.

- An accountant can also register you or the business for tax with HMRC and deal with HMRC on your behalf as your tax agent.

- Obtaining advice enables you to run the business tax efficiently and make savings. Outsourcing certain tasks saves time, so you can concentrate on running your business.

- Useful websites:

    - https://www.gov.uk/browse/business

    - https://www.gov.uk/topic/business-tax/self-employed

    - http://www.startupdonut.co.uk/

    - http://www.taxdonut.co.uk/

* Figures based on the tax year 6 April 2016 to 5 April 2017.

This information has been prepared by Chipperfield Accounting Ltd for information purposes only and cannot be relied upon to make business decisions. Readers are recommended to obtain bespoke advice applicable to their individual circumstances before setting up a new business. Tax rates and tax treatment are subject to change. Chipperfield Accounting Ltd bears no responsibility for any loss suffered as a result of reliance being placed on the information provided.

Mumpreneur Case Study – Website design business with no business plan! ★

Susie Tobias, Wise Genius – age 44, with daughter aged 15 and son aged 13.

What does your business do?

I started Wise Genius in 2010 and I design and build websites for small businesses, specialising in the application of the WordPress content management system. I also provide website support services and consultancy.

What motivated you to start your business?

After having my daughter in 2001, I knew that I didn't want to return to an office-based job or one in my previous career, town planning. I hadn't considered working for myself until my husband set up his own business in 2008. By that time, I had two children and felt even further away from getting back into traditional employment. I had been working on a voluntary basis for a web-based business, Netmums, since 2002, and had started doing a web design course via a distance-learning company. I was equipped with the tools to build websites for other people, yet none of the confidence. I was lucky enough to meet two enterprising ladies who had set up a networking group. They asked me to redesign their website, which provided the springboard for working with other members of the group and setting up Wise Genius. I had found something that I enjoyed and people who were willing to pay me to do it for them.

What mistakes did you make when you set up your business?

Too many to mention! I think the most obvious was that I didn't have a clear business plan or an idea of who I wanted to work with – I took on every piece of work that came my way!

How do you juggle family and business?

I set clear boundaries between work and family time. I start work as soon as the kids have left the house at 8am each morning and finish once they are both home, usually around 4pm. I may work up until 5pm, however I make this clear to the children and don't expect to be disturbed. I will only work in the evening or weekends on very rare occasions. All this means that I must be disciplined with my time. Of course, one benefit for working for myself from home is that I can attend day-based school events or be there if the kids are sick. I am also able to share these duties with my husband who also works from home.

What are your future plans for your business?

I am looking to build a team of associates around me to provide complementary services to my clients. My big dream is to leave my desk in the corner of the dining room and have my own office.

Susie added: 'Don't wait for the perfect moment to start your business, just get going. You are bound to make mistakes – learn from them. Being in business is a constant learning process – embrace it.'

Chapter 7

MARKETING & SALES

What is marketing? The definition is: *'The action or business of promoting and selling products or services, including market research and advertising.'*

Most small businesses and startups I work with never start in the right place and that is with a plan! A marketing plan is vital to success and will include the audience you are targeting, the channels you will use and what your budget is.

Website

A website is ***vital***. All businesses need an online presence and I would highly recommend getting a website at the start. I have worked with businesses that just use a Facebook page to start off with, however, this isn't what I recommend! My view is owning your own website and domain name is vital for long-term success and remember if you ever want to sell the business then all you build up is part of the IP of the business.

Who is your ideal client?

- Know your ideal client and understand their problems and pain points!

- Think about what they wear, what they do for a living, where they spend their spare time, what car they drive and where they live.

- What problems does your business solve?

- Think about your business from your customer's point of view.

- Emotion – think...

Who, What, When, Where, Why & How

Brainstorm this in your notebook:

- Who are you aiming at?

- What are you selling them?

- When will they buy it?

- Where will they buy it?

- Why will they buy it?

- How will they buy it?

This is what you need to include in your plan:

✓ Carry out a SWOT – your strengths, weaknesses, opportunities and threats.

I think this is such a useful exercise. Spend time really thinking about all these aspects.

Strengths – could be your experience, qualifications and skills. Could also be where you are based. May also be your team. Could be the money you have to invest.

Weaknesses – what do you need help with? May be some of what I have mentioned above.

Opportunities – could be places or people to promote your business, shows and exhibitions, perhaps a new housing estate is being built in your area, or new government legislation.

Threats – do competitor research, although they might be an opportunity rather than a threat; think of strategic alliances and consider things that may cause problems in your business.

- ✓ Objectives – what do you want to achieve e.g. new clients, more clients, higher spend from existing clients, retain existing clients, referrals.

  In year 1 your objective will be clients but think about how you are going to retain people from the start and look after them!

- ✓ Budget – how much do you want to spend on marketing? This includes networking, printing, promotional goods, advertising.

- ✓ Profile your competitors – what are they offering? You may have done this on the SWOT, but I think it warrants full research and this could also be contacting companies out of the area.

- ✓ How can you raise your profile? e.g. awards, charity projects, blogs, events.

- ✓ Make an annual schedule – list an activity and topics for each month of the year. This will create focus.

Write your plan, research every available marketing opportunity in your area: Networking, Chamber of Commerce, Enterprise Agency, local magazines, leaflet drops, events. Consider what may work for your business but you need to get out there and talk to people.

My A-Z of marketing channels you can try

The decision about which of these to try depends on your business. Do more research on each and decide which ones you will try. Measure the effectiveness of each one over at least three months.

Add on to existing clients – sell other goods or services to existing clients.

Advertising – paid advertisements in magazines and newspapers. These are usually expensive and, in most cases, can be ineffective. Find out the distribution, call other advertisers and decide if your target market will read this.

Awards – many have a new business category, great for PR if you win or are a finalist.

Blogging – post on a regular basis, weekly is ideal, monthly is the minimum. Talk about ideas which solve the problems your customers have. Give away some valuable content.

Books – write a book or an ebook, share your knowledge and showcase your expertise in your field.

Case studies – use these from your customers to add to your website, social media, blog and YouTube.

Cold calling – this does work for some business types. Buy a reputable list – do not just pick off companies at random online.

Customer retention – look after the customers you gain. Set up referral schemes, keep in touch and give them special offers for repeat business.

Email marketing – investigate email software options such as MailChimp, Constant Contact. Send out regular offers and updates. Buy lists only from reputable companies. Have a list-building plan. Make sure you are compliant with data protection law, see www.ico.org.uk

Exhibitions and events – find local events and get involved by having a stand or visiting. This is a great way to build your brand and meet new people. Could you organise an event of your own to showcase your business?

Facebook – build a Facebook page, learn how to do Facebook Ads well. Most businesses in the B2C market benefit hugely from Facebook but make sure you learn how to do it right!

Google – set up a Google business account. Google Places will help you get found so make sure your website is optimised for Google search. Set up Google Alerts for key words to see what is being talked about online. Investigate Google Adwords – this might be right for your business. Make sure your website has Google Analytics installed. This is so you can monitor the traffic to your website; this will help you understand how your website is working for you.

Instagram – if you have a product-based business this may work well for you.

LinkedIn – a good profile well optimised goes a long way. If you are aiming at business-to business customers, then make sure you get proper training to use this site effectively.

Mail out – send something through the post. This can be expensive but with the right list and the right item sent this can be very productive because people don't get much mail anymore! So, consider a coloured envelope, something interesting inside and information that is relevant to the person you are sending it to. Again, buy a good list.

Networking – see page 118 on this.

Outdoor ads – you can advertise on buses, bus stops, shop windows and billboards. If you are using a venue you may be allowed to put up a banner outside.

Partnerships – are there other companies you can do partnerships with?

Pinterest – social media platform built around sharing images, so excellent for you if you have a business which has great images to share.

Print and promotional items – consider carefully what you need. Most leaflet drops are a waste of money, but for some companies it does work particularly well e.g. gardening and cleaning services, fast food and restaurants.

PR and press releases – if you have a newsworthy story see if you can get some press coverage. Talk to a PR agency and get their view. Try sending a press release to your local paper or magazines. Make sure you have a story, they are not interested in an advert but news. Tweet a taste of your story to #JournoRequest on Twitter and check the feed on this hashtag for journalists appealing for stories on a particular subject. You may fit the bill!

Public speaking – you can raise your profile by offering to speak at networking events, industry events and local groups such as Rotary or Women's Institute. Check out the PSA (Public Speaking Association) or Toastmaster groups for help on public speaking. I can also recommend a book by Dee Clayton *Taming Your Public Speaking Monkeys: A Guide to Confidence Building for Presentations.*

Referral programme – get existing clients or business associates to pass you leads. If they translate to paid business, offer them an incentive.

SEO – get specialist advice and check out the information in this book for basic advice.

Snap Chat – if your business is aimed at the under 21s this may be a useful platform to advertise on.

Sponsorship – can you sponsor an event, a team or something which gives your business prominence to your target market?

Twitter – microblogging site, depends on your business whether it will be effective and the time you spend using it.

Website – see my top tips on building a website. You need a website – period!

YouTube – upload useful content, tag it and promote via social media.

This list is not exhaustive but gives you a lot of options to try. For further reading these are some books I recommend:

Geoff Ramm, *(OMG) Observational Marketing Greats*

Dee Blick, *The Ultimate Small Business Marketing Book* and *Powerful Marketing on a Shoestring Budget: For Small Businesses*

Bryony Thomas, *Watertight Marketing*

Outsourcing your marketing

Most startups do not consider this, however here are some reasons you might want to consider if you have some capital or once you have an income coming in.

If you find you are spending more time on your marketing instead of your workload it may be more cost-effective to outsource it. This will allow you to focus on your customers, increase business sales and improve your business profile.

If you don't understand how to measure what is working and what isn't, get some advice otherwise you will waste money.

If you lack ideas and inspiration and your efforts aren't producing any results this doesn't mean the business isn't working, this means the marketing isn't working – so, get professional help before you throw in the towel. You can benefit from objective, honed advice insights and ideas you may never have thought of. A marketing expert will give you an edge over your competitors.

If you need to gain knowledge about social media there are tons of training courses out there both face to face and online – get help! You will get a return on your investment working with an expert who can support you to deliver targeted campaigns and strategy.

And as I said earlier – at the very least do your research and **get a marketing plan completed!**

Marketing trends – what should you be doing?

- Live video – Facebook Live

- Video sharing – YouTube Channel

- Visual = quick, absorbable and easy content

- Mobile applications

- Develop your business with the next generation in mind

- People want to be educated and not have your business pushed at them

- Engagement and education and use # hashtags

Focus on the problems you solve and share your expertise.

Website tips

Be wary of building your site in a cheap platform yourself. If you do, make sure you pay for the add-on services otherwise your website will be hidden.

You can build your own site via WordPress and there are other sites which offer a self-build service. But if you don't have the time or are not technical then consider these points when asking someone to build a website:

- Use someone reputable and check their work first
- Look at a few sites you like and decide how you want yours to function
- Always think of the customer
- Make sure the home page looks good, has social media buttons and a place for people to sign up to your email list. The email list you build is vital to your marketing

Have the following pages:

- About you
- Your products and services
- Contact us
- You may wish to add a news page/blog
- Have social media share buttons on each page
- Video

Get expert help with your website, marketing, social media and SEO.

Cheryl Luzet from Wagada, a Mumpreneur herself, shares these top SEO tips to get your website found

Getting your website ranked on Google as a small business can seem like an impossible task when there are so many competitors with seemingly big budgets. But there are many things that small businesses can do themselves to boost their search engine ranking, as well as convert more of the people who land on the website.

Over the past few years securing conversions and providing a strong user experience has become more important to Google – it wants the top-ranking websites to meet the needs of their users. We need to demonstrate to search engines that your website provides the best experience. The site needs to be easy to use, full of interesting, engaging and informative content, relevant to the keywords that people are searching and popular enough for other people on the web to want to talk about you and link to you.

Make sure that you have enough content on your website to engage and interest your visitors. Some people are afraid to add content as it doesn't look as pretty as images – but if you have nothing to say on your website you can't demonstrate engagement to Google.

Here are our top tips for boosting your search engine ranking:

1. **Add lots of high-quality, unique content regularly, Google loves fresh content!**

   The more (high-quality) content on a website, the more likely it will get found. So, get writing. Aim to add something new to your site at least every month.

2. **Length**

   Currently, Google favours long form content – so 500 to 1,500 words. Yes 1,500 words! Particularly for the longer, more niche keyword phrases, Google is ranking the web pages which are more comprehensive and longer. Longer content makes more use of the keyword phrases, looks more relevant and more informative. However, large paragraphs of content can be off-putting – so do consider how you present this long content to make it easy to read and scan on the web.

3. **Topic tips**

When choosing your topic, think about the keyword phrase that you would like the page to rank for. Web searchers tend to search their *problem*, rather than the *solution* – so think about the sorts of problems that your target audience could be facing. What questions could they be asking? Make a note of the questions that your clients ask you – these make fabulous blog titles. The website Answer the Public is a great source of questions that people are asking on the web and good for generating ideas for keywords and blog topics for your own sites.

4. **Don't forget your meta descriptions**

The meta description is the small paragraph of content which appears in search results – it is your opportunity to tell people what your website is about and why they should click on your listing. Google won't always show the meta description that you select, as sometimes it prefers to make up its own, but if you do have a strong compelling description it is more likely to display yours. Lots of companies don't write their own meta descriptions, they let the web designer fill in this section for them. This is such a wasted opportunity to engage your target audience. Write the meta description at the same time that you write the content for your website.

5. Presentation – make it easy to read

No one likes to be faced with a long chunk of content on the web – it's hard to read and it's off-putting. We are all rather impatient and task orientated on the web – so we have a tendency to scan rather than read web pages.

So, make your content easy to digest and scan:

- Split longer content into short paragraphs/bitesize chunks

- Write in accessible language with shorter sentences that are easy to follow on a screen

- Use sub-headings to make scanning easier

- Don't forget white space – you're not short of space so spread it out

- Use images to split the content up and make it more engaging

- Bullet points split out the content and make it obvious that we are listing several points. Easier to scan too!

6. Spice it up with strong images

Use images to bring the article to life and make it more engaging. They illustrate the text and make scanning easier. When you save the image prior to uploading it, think about the keyword you are writing the content around and include it in the filename of the image before you upload. This will help Google to understand what the image is about. Also, don't forget to include your keyword in your ALT tags. The purpose of ALT tags is to describe the image to blind people – so don't forget to also make sure that the ALT tag properly describes the image.

7. Don't copy or duplicate your content please!

Don't be tempted to copy content from another site. Google does not like duplicate content, and while it won't directly penalise you, it can decide not to include pages of duplicate content in its index – so it won't rank when people search for that phrase.

8. Don't be afraid to link out

Make your content look more informative and useful to Google by linking out to authoritative sources. Links out were once considered bad, but now Google favours articles which link out as they make the article look more useful and informative.

9. Internal links

Link internally within your website to other relevant articles. This helps Google to see how these topics are related. It also encourages readers to view other pages of your website, which can send positive user signals to Google. The more engaging the site, the more pages that people will visit – so let's show the search engines how engaging our content is. Think about the text that you include in the link – called the anchor text. Using phrases which relate to the keywords of the page that you are linking to can help reinforce its relevance.

It can be hard to find the time to invest in our websites, but they are so crucial to the success of a business. Try and set aside a couple of hours each week to update the content and make improvements to your website as regular updates will have more benefit than adding a lot of content in one go. Google likes to see that a website is being lovingly maintained and so will your customers.

Mumpreneur Case Study ★

Cheryl Luzet, Wagada Ltd, she has two children and started her business in 2011.

What motivated you to start your business?

After child number two I calculated the cost of childcare and when added to the cost of my train fare into London I worked out I would have a take-home pay of £5 a day after tax. I was in the Catch 22 situation that many women find themselves in where they cannot afford to give up work, but they cannot afford to work. My husband is a teacher, so he does not have a big salary, so I knew I would have to try to find an income. I had always wanted to run my own business but had never had the guts to give up a steady salary to try it out – this was my opportunity to find out if I could do it.

What mistakes did you make when you set up your business?

I waited too long to take on my first member of staff and worked myself into the ground in the process. I had been working at home with no overheads so employing staff changes everything – I had to take on an office and responsibilities. But once you take that step it is very rewarding and secures the future of your business and allows you to grow. I didn't have the confidence in myself that I could have a grown-up business with an office and overheads.

How do you juggle family and business?

My son was only nine months old when I set my business up. I paid for childcare at least a few days a week right from the beginning. This was difficult as it was an expensive outlay and for the first few months I was paying more in childcare than I was earning. But without it I would never have been able to grow my business at the speed that I did. Now the children are at school I am able to be flexible, and catch up the extra hours early morning, or in the evenings or at the weekend.

What are your future plans for your business?

I now have a team of nine employed staff and am happy with the size of the business. In recent years we have expanded our range of services to offer both offline and online marketing. We have recently changed our target audience away from micro businesses to larger organisations with bigger budgets. This will allow us to offer a more rounded service and achieve better results.

Anything else you want to add?

Constantly re-evaluate what you are doing and how you do it. The best businesses are flexible to their outside environment and not constricted by inflexible plans. You need a strategic direction, but you don't need very firm long-term plans as long as you are constantly reassessing what you are doing and if it is taking you in the direction that you would like to go.

Building an email list

In my view it's important you build a subscriber list. There are two main reasons:

1. You can keep in regular touch with people who are interested in your goods or services and add value to them by offering them discounts, new product information and valuable tips.

2. If you lose your Facebook page (yes, they do shut them down) you will still have your client data.

To keep your hard-earned subscribers do not bombard them. Set up expectations from the start. My company Mums UnLtd sends an email to anyone who subscribes which says: 'We will email you weekly with our list of events' – this means they know they will get emails each week and what I am emailing them. So, if I sent them random emails selling products they would unsubscribe as this is not what they were expecting. Never pass on their details to anyone else.

Make sure you communicate regularly – if you allow this list to gather dust people will forget who you are!

From Zero to Hero! How can you grow your list?

- When anyone buys from you get their details and get their permission to email them.

- Have a capture form on your website. I use Mail Munch which pops up and allows people to get the information on events. You might want to add an offer as an incentive.

- The best way to increase your list is to provide great value and make people think they will miss out if they are not on your list!

- Tell them they will be the first to get information on offers and to try new products or services.

Give people a gift for signing up – here are some ideas:

1. Ebook – tips, how to's around your topics and their pain points

2. Cheat sheet/checklists/workbooks/ideas list – people love these

3. Webinar/video/class (live or pre-recorded)

4. Some kind of planner

5. Discount codes/money off voucher

6. A bundle/pack on a particular topic

Make sure that what you offer is genuinely useful; I see so much rubbish offered and have signed up to oodles of crap over my time in business. The content must be directed at your target market and it must be relevant to them and solve a problem they have. Make sure you consider the format. For example, a webinar lasting an hour without a recording may not be suitable for people who are time poor!

Segment your list

I have worked with tons of businesses that have never segmented their list! Make sure you come up with a plan *from the start*. For example, you could segment by customer type, area in which they live or what products they have bought. By doing this the emails you send will be relevant and you will get less unsubscribes.

For example:

- For people who have signed up to your list but never purchased you may wish to send an introductory offer

- For those who have purchased something, an offer of something else and refer to the original purchase

For Mums UnLtd our list is segmented by area because we send out emails about our events. There is little point in sending the events in Hertfordshire to those in Whitstable in Kent!

Track and measure campaigns

Check your open rates, understand who is unsubscribing, check who is opening what links. This will tell you if people are interested in what you are saying! Don't add too much information to the email – link it into the website. You want traffic to your website.

Make sure you are compliant with data protection when sending emails, check www.ico.org.uk

Launch event

I love a good launch event and it surprises me the number of small businesses that never bother with this. This doesn't need to cost a fortune and it depends what business you have – but consider it!

My top 10 tips are:

1. Hold it somewhere which is relevant to your business.

2. Invite prospective customers along. LinkedIn, Twitter and Facebook are valuable for finding the right target audience to invite.

3. Attend some networking events and invite the people you meet.

4. Contact your local Chamber of Commerce and get them involved.

5. Invite local VIPs e.g. local mayor, local councillor, local MP, local celebrities.

6. Make sure you call your local radio station and your nearest BBC station. I have been on the radio many times talking about my business.

7. Invite your local paper and send a press release.

8. Invite companies that would be potential joint ventures and partners.

9. Get involved with a local charity that would make a good link with what you are doing, invite them along and hold a raffle for them.

10. Share on social media, before, during and after the event with videos and photos.

Networking

Networking is the most powerful business tool. It is by far the best way to form lasting business relationships.

This is such a big subject and one people often get so wrong. I could have written a book just about networking, but I decided that there were enough of those out there already (see further reading) and my aim was to write a book to inspire people to run a business around their family rather than do a job they hate or do nothing.

It is a fact that 70% of all new business is gained through word of mouth and positive recommendation. People will pass business to those they know, like and trust. This comes with time and practice!

Attending business networking events raises your company profile, people will learn about your business and what you do. They will also find out what services you offer and what you can do to help.

Building a network with reliable contacts is vitally important. You don't know who you don't know! So, you never know when a contact will be useful and present you with new opportunities. Restricting the level of contacts you have will limit those opportunities. Connecting with like-minded individuals can be important for ideas, support, sharing problems and success.

Most people don't network with purpose. One of the most common mistakes is that they don't follow up properly. They go to a meeting, collect a few cards and add them to their database. They might make a 1-2-1 appointment but most don't. This is ineffective and won't help your business much, if at all.

Networking can help you build a team of experts around your business. All of my team have come from networking, so from graphic design, website design, copywriting, printing, my VA and even the publisher of this book! All of these people I met at networking events.

Business networking helps you to improve your communication skills. It is a great confidence booster. Helping others is also very satisfying. People you help will always remember you.

Here are my top 15 tips:

1. **Do your research**

   With so many networking events you need to find what works for you. You also must know the rules, know the organisers and the key people. Know what they offer and how they can help you.

   BNI (Business Network International) tend to run breakfast meetings at 6.30am although in some areas they do lunchtime meetings. They are weekly, you are committed to attend each week and the cost is around £700 for membership plus your weekly fee.

There are female networking groups which meet monthly at lunchtimes: check out WIBN, Athena Networking, 1230 Women's Club. These all have a membership and you pay for the lunches. I have given you contact details at the back of the book. There are also groups aimed at mums which are usually at 930am for two hours. My company Mums UnLtd has a number of groups but there are also lots of companies offering something similar across the UK. Best place to check is Google.

2. Don't expect too much too soon

When you join a networking group don't expect too much in the first few months. It does take time to get to know people, build relationships and trust before people will refer business to you. Focus on the support and advice of other business owners you are receiving; there is a wealth of knowledge and experience at every event you attend.

3. Understand your fellow networkers

Once you begin to understand your fellow networkers and their needs, you can begin to think about how you can help them. If you get that right, you'll get lots of help in return.

4. Keep commitments

Always do what you say you are going to do. Keep to commitments. It is surprising how many times people promise to call or email and they don't! Networking circles are actually quite small, and word will get around if someone proves to be unreliable.

5. Follow up referrals

Following through with what you say you will do earns you the respect of others; failing to do something loses it very quickly. Always follow through any referral anyone gives you quickly, ideally within 24 hours. They are putting their reputation on the line by passing it to you. Always update with an outcome and a thank you.

6. **Arrange 1-2-1s and connect on social media**

The actual networking events are just a small part of networking. They are merely an introduction session and if you only attend events and do nothing else, nothing will happen.

Anyone you meet could be a good contact for you: you don't know who they know, where they have worked or who they do business with. Don't disregard anyone. Through making conversation and taking the time to develop relationships you will find connections that lead to business.

As you need to ensure you are working and generating income you need to decide how much time you will spend each month/week on 1-2-1s with people you meet. Be more effective by targeting contacts in your group who provide obvious strategic alliances. For example:

Massage therapist / osteopath / beautician / fitness trainer / weight loss consultant: they are all coming in contact with people concerned about their health and wellbeing.

Solicitor/accountant/financial adviser: they are all coming in contact with people to do with financial issues.

Then you need to think about making connections with people who are not so obvious.

Make up a spreadsheet and list the types of professions that would make good contacts for you. Then list people you have met and arrange to meet with them. Keep an ongoing record of what you have done, plan to do and the results.

Think also about your hobbies and interests; key relationships can be formed from this. Who else that you have met likes playing golf, attending the theatre or some other sport or hobby you could share?

Pick two people you meet per event you attend and get a date in the diary to meet them, three if you can. Then spend one hour with that person, 30 minutes on each business. Ask lots of questions, find out what they do, what help they need and what makes them tick! Then follow up after this meeting with ideas and contacts. Or how about arranging a skill swap?

7. Use LinkedIn, Twitter and Facebook

Use these to connect with people you meet and people who have attended events you didn't get the chance to speak to. Use the lists that are sent out from events to do this and to make connections with people who you haven't met but would be mutually beneficial.

8. A minute to win it!

Many networking groups ask you to do a one-minute introduction at the meeting, sometimes called an elevator pitch. Preparing this means you can be clear on what you do and what help you are asking for and then you don't confuse people or waffle. The elevator pitch should be around one minute, and this is approximately 200 words. Write three or four versions and practise them.

Asking for specific business rather than listing all of your services will get you more success. Be clear, be concise. Think about who you can help. Who is your target market? You can also promote a key service each month or special offer. A song, prop, photographs, poem or a testimonial can be a great way to be remembered. If you are attending the same group each week try to be inventive and creative, otherwise you can come across as boring! Don't attempt all of these at once, just one idea at a time!

9. **Set up your own team to help you with your business**

If you work in a large company you have a marketing department, HR, Finance, IT and a social life. If you are a sole trader or small company, you can find out who is in your network that can supply these services to you, or that fellow networkers recommend. Larger companies can look to partner with companies who can refer business to them – setting up discounts or affiliates schemes.

10. **Attend networking events regularly – be a known face**

Going to an event on a regular basis means you will get known and people are more likely to refer business to someone they know, they like, and they trust. Going to a meeting once is unlikely to get you business, you must be a regular face. If you get business the first time you go to an event, this is luck! But don't over network. You know you are over networking when you don't have the time to do 1-2-1s and follow ups. You have to manage your time between work, networking and 1-2-1s.

11. **Ask for testimonials**

Use on your website, LinkedIn, Facebook, literature and verbally ask people to recommend you at events.

12. **Give testimonials**

An email takes five minutes to do but can make a big difference.

13. **Ensure you have clear literature**

This means good quality business cards and leaflets.

14. A website

Over 80% of people look online for the services they need, so ensure you have a good clear site which is easy to use. Link this with all your social media activities. People you meet at events will check this.

15. Always be smart and presentable

You are your shop window!

Follow up – always. It amazes me how many people never bother.

Networking with children!

This isn't easy as it's hard to focus on your business with children running around, however there are groups that allow this but consider also attending one that is child free. This will give you head space and some time to focus on your business.

Use networking to build your social media tribe

You must have a strong social media presence to be successful in business today. Whether it's Twitter, Facebook or LinkedIn, you can connect online with people that have a common interest on the other side of the world. Offer something of value on their Facebook page or Twitter stream. It's a small connect but it is often noticed and valued. However, these are weak ties, you don't know them, you have never met them, this relationship isn't personal.

By supporting people online that you know, like and trust from networking events you are adding massive value to their business and their bottom line.

It's so powerful! Your endorsement of them on social media is worth so much!

Here are some ideas of what you can do to support fellow networkers and what they can do to support you back.

Social media

Facebook

In the third quarter of 2016, Facebook had 1.79 billion monthly active users – you cannot ignore this!

The average user has 338 friends on Facebook – this means if you are a regular at a group with 20 people and they agree to like, comment or share one of your posts per month, you have a potential reach of 6,760 people! This is free! So, take action:

- ✓ Like each other's business pages
- ✓ Comment and share information in groups
- ✓ Friend each other
  - Commenting and sharing helps massively – a 'Like' is OK but better results are driven by comments and shares

You can use each other's content, which helps when thinking about what to share on your page.

LinkedIn

There are well over 467 million users on LinkedIn. Everyone who has a business should have a profile, as Google will index it and it helps with SEO. LinkedIn is basically a huge database! You can search for people by industry, location and company name. By connecting with the people you meet networking you then become a second degree connection of everyone they are connected to – giving you reach into millions!

The average person has 930 people on LinkedIn and so therefore on average this will put 930 into your network, plus then their connections will become your third degree! More if you connect with people who have a larger connection base.

- ✓ Connect with people you meet on LinkedIn, check the stream, like comment and share their updates
- ✓ Post updates about your business, blogs and share information that you think is useful

Twitter

There are 317 million active users and this site is great for sharing a bit of quick info, a photo or short video!

- ✓ Follow each other, use lists to monitor and retweet good info and comment when applicable
- ✓ Use your phone – the app makes it quick and easy to do – I spend some time while the kettle boils!
- ✓ Use # for key words

Instagram

There are over 800 million active users, now owned by Facebook; 20% of internet users use Instagram.

A photo and video sharing site – use # for key words.

- ✓ Use phone app for easy updating and following
- ✓ Used a lot in health, beauty, fashion industry and for a younger audience but lots of older people are now using it.

Boost your presence through the people you meet

- ✓ Use your face to face networking to boost your social media presence by people who know you, who are more likely to want to help you and who trust you enough to recommend you to their family and friends

✓ Leave recommendations for each other when you have used someone's services, either on Facebook or LinkedIn – these are valuable

Build a strong network

Build your network to be stronger and deeper; many people make the mistake of going to lots of events, they flit from one to another and don't spend enough time making meaningful relationships. This is a mistake so many people make!

Building a successful and sustainable business takes effort and part of that is building great rapport and a fantastic reputation with people in your local area.

Social media content ideas

What is valuable and relevant content?

You need to understand your customers in order to anticipate the kind of things they want:

- Valuable

- Very useful/important

- Relevant

- Closely connected

This allows your audience to share with their audience and will entice new followers – potential customers. Become a thought leader/expert in your field.

Post ideas

✓ Conversations with members of your audience and professionals in your niche

- ✓ Trending topics in your field
- ✓ Case studies
- ✓ Reviews of products (books, tools, software)
- ✓ Responses to articles posted on other blogs
- ✓ Weekly curation of the best content found on a specific topic
- ✓ Tutorials /how-to's
- ✓ Lists of your favourite tools, resources, blogs, brands
- ✓ Positive lessons learned from challenging experiences
- ✓ Interviews of specialists in your niche
- ✓ Infographics
- ✓ Highlight of the best comments your blog has received
- ✓ Helpful tips, including insider secrets
- ✓ Roundup of your most popular posts to date
- ✓ Series of short articles centred around a specific topic
- ✓ Roundup of best tips shared by your favourite experts
- ✓ Recurring mistakes you see in your industry
- ✓ Repurposing of old content into different formats (slide decks, videos, infographics, podcasts)

Lead conversion

All the information shared in this chapter is designed to generate more leads for your business. However, unless you can sell, those leads will be wasted. Sales is the process of converting your leads into a purchasing customer. There are massive differences in how you will convert leads for products and services.

My top tips are:

- ✓ Sales start with a conversation and rapport building. Speak to your prospect – this is ideal for a service-based business. So, get an appointment in the diary to either speak on the phone or for a face to face meeting. Then use these questions to qualify a potential customer.

Qualification questions

- ✓ Is there a genuine business problem or need that our solution will address?
- ✓ Who is getting the pain from the problem?
- ✓ What would it be worth to the client to have a solution?
- ✓ What budget does the client have?
- ✓ What is the problem costing them, in actual loss, lost opportunity or untapped discretionary effort?
- ✓ Then, really, what budget does the client have?
- ✓ Is anybody else competing with us for this?
- ✓ What other value can we add using our creativity in service to the client? (secondary benefits and exceeding expectation)
- ✓ How will the client expect success to be measured?
- ✓ Is there a strategic advantage to acquiring this client? e.g. brand
- ✓ Will this business be profitable for us?
- ✓ What are the benefits/risks? (scope creep!)
- ✓ Will the engagement result in a satisfied client and repeat business?

- ✓ Is the client willing to be a case study/advocate or give you a testimonial?

- ✓ Listen to your prospective customer – what do they want and need and what is their budget?

- ✓ Ask lots of questions to help qualify them and get to know and understand them.

When selling products it's always about the features and benefits and make sure you are clear on what problems you solve or why your product stands out in the marketplace.

Having good testimonials is vital as you can share satisfied customers with your prospects. Video is ideal and people enthusing about your business will sell this to potential customers!

Make ordering and paying for your product or service easy. Test the buying process and get others to do the same. You can easily lose sales from a website which isn't very user friendly or from staff who are poorly trained.

Check out these books on sales. This is a vast subject I have only briefly touched on. So, you will find additional reading on this topic really useful.

Agile Selling – Jill Konrath

The 7 Habits of Highly Effective People – Stephen Covey

The Psychology of Selling – Brian Tracy

Power of Influence – Robert Cialdini

Customer retention – once you have the clients, now what?

It's important to consider how you will look after your clients. If you do a great job or sell them a great product, although a happy customer does not guarantee repurchase it plays a really important part in ensuring customer loyalty and retention. You should always strive for excellence in customer service. You want to ensure they refer you to other people and that they give you a great review! Also consider the following:

1. **What additional revenues can you create to add more to your bottom line from your existing clients?** Sometimes called the upsell, we can often sell more to clients who already work with us.

2. **How will you keep in contact with your clients from the very start?** Consider a regular email update, phone calls or cards when you think they might need your products or services again.

3. **Put in place a referral system.** If a customer recommends you, send them a thank you, a gift or a discount. This rewards them and makes them feel valued.

4. **How will you retain clients?** You will only retain clients if you look after them. The process will depend on what you sell or service you offer. Think about what you think they might need, e.g. an out of hours number, a call-back service when lines are busy, a phone answering service when you are busy or online booking or re-ordering system.

5. **What added value can you give your clients which will cost you very little?** Sometimes it's the little things that mean a lot!

TAKE ACTION

Chapter 7 covered masses of information, the main points to remember are:

- ✓ Work out who you are targeting
- ✓ Complete a marketing plan – choosing your channels carefully
- ✓ Monitor your marketing by making sure you know where the leads are coming from
- ✓ Work on your lead conversions

Chapter 8

PROCESSES

Designing efficient processes is a key part of setting up a business. All too often I meet Mumpreneurs who have bits of information in files, some in Excel and some in their head! This is not the way to run a business and you will quickly come unstuck.

You must build a business that has clear processes on how you deal with your customers, record your transactions, manage your marketing, design your sales process and deliver your product or service. By doing this you will have a business that you can grow and maybe one day sell.

So where do you start?

Think about the customer first and their journey to buy from you. Do people want to be messing around sending emails and bank transfers to pay for your goods or services?

No they don't!

It's all about simplicity. Search, Click and Pay.

For example, I was working with a children's language school that had classes listed on their website. To book a class you had to call and then transfer the money by BACS. Invoices were raised in Excel.

Here are the problems:

- People may be searching for what you do late at night and early in the morning because they cannot call during working hours

- People are busy, and they want the flexibility to do transactions when it suits them

- They find out once they call that the classes are full – disappointing and annoying

- If other classes are offering online availability and payment online this puts your competitors ahead of you

- If competitors are not offering this, you are then ahead

- If invoicing is automated when a client makes a booking this means no manual invoicing, makes keeping accounting easier

- Chasing payments is time consuming and taking cheques to the bank or checking the banking system for payments; getting immediate payment is great for your cash flow

Here is the solution:

- There are cheap plug-ins for WordPress (I use Event Manager Pro) to enable customers to book online and check availability of spaces

- This links with PayPal (and other payment portals)

- This interfaces with Kashflow, my accounting system (and other payment portals)

- This means clients can confirm a space, book, pay and the accounting is done at any time of day or night

- More time can then be spent on other tasks such as marketing!

Setting processes at the start will save you time and money and, in my experience, help you grow your business quicker and with more professionalism.

You also want a system for collecting customer information. It's so important to profile your customers and this will assist in your marketing and help you to provide them with the goods or services they need. Collect as much information as you can at the point of sale. This includes their personal data and email. Then use a system to record when they purchased and what they purchased.

Use this information to look after your customers. You could send birthday cards, personal recommendations for products and services, and keep track of when they are likely to purchase again.

For example, if you sell print to customers, such as business cards and leaflets, you can work out when they are likely to need more and send them an email reminder to re-order their business cards or leaflets. This works with any business. You can ask them to leave you reviews, suggest your service to friends and use their email data for marketing, not just email marketing but on Facebook.

If you do not have processes early on to do this then you will be left with a mess! I have worked with many businesses that have no clear record system or processes and they are literally leaving money on the table.

Data protection

Making sure you have clear processes in place for handling customer data is vital. There are hefty fines for businesses that breach these laws. As a business you will handle all manner of customer data and it's vital you know exactly how to do this. You must familiarise yourself on the data protection laws. Check out all the latest information at https://www.gov.uk/data-protection. And also check this page: https://ico.org.uk/for-organisations/guide-to-data-protection/key-definitions/

As this is changing, my advice is to read these websites. A few key things to remember are to ensure all customer data is encrypted, that you do not keep data any longer than is necessary and you must have consent to add people to your email lists. But there are a number of other things you should be aware of and it depends on what you do and what data you use, so make sure you check the pages I mentioned.

Expert advice

I asked expert process manager, Carli Wall from Synergy Business Support, to share the best online tools for an efficient business.

Online tools for an efficient business

There are many online tools available for creating a more efficient business. These are my top picks of business processes to streamline (including suggestions for the service to use), to help you save time or make tasks easier. Some of them may seem unnecessary; however, think about when you are busier or perhaps want someone to take over some tasks for you.

Cloud storage and filing - Google Drive, One Drive, Dropbox

Useful if you regularly work on documents with a client. No need to keep emailing documents, keeping your files in 'the cloud' means you will always see the latest document, can see previous versions and who made changes, and you can share them with other people for viewing or editing.

Appointment scheduling - Acuity, Calendly, Vcita, Set More

Set up a calendar with the times you are available and send a link that people can use to book themselves in to one of your available slots.

CRM system - Capsule, Zoho, Insightly, Hubspot

Store the data of your clients, prospects and contacts, much like a lot of people do in a spreadsheet, but you can also record notes, details of discussions, calls and meetings you've had, what services they used, rates you gave them, where the business came from and so much more.

Accounts - Freshbooks, Xero, QuickBooks, Kashflow, Free Agent

Quick and easy invoicing with reminders sent for outstanding invoices, so less time chasing payments. Enter your expenses, receipts and mileage from an app on your phone.

Forms and surveys - Google Forms, Survey Monkey, Jotform

Collect information that you need to get from enquiries or clients, plus feedback and testimonials. Set up one form, or a suite of different forms you will need, send out a link to it and the other person fills it in online and the information comes back to you.

Task management - Trello, Asana, Teamwork, Todoist

Manage and track your tasks or projects so you can see what you need to do and when. Especially useful if you are using it to work with a team or your clients, as everyone can see who is responsible for which tasks.

Emails - MailChimp, MailerLite, Aweber, Constant Contact, Active Campaign

Create email sequences to be delivered in a set order at set intervals, useful for when new people sign up to your list, or for delivering information for training or programmes. Also useful for delivering an attachment or download for people that have signed up to your list in order to receive a particular ebook, checklist, or other opt in 'freebie'.

Agreements and contracts - Signable, Adobe Sign, Right Signature

Send an agreement and have it back to you signed in minutes, instead of sending hard copies of agreements through the post for signing, or emailing it to the other person and having them scan it back to you with their signature on.

Social media - Hootsuite, Buffer, Meet Edgar, Postplanner, Facebook scheduling

Schedule your posts and updates in advance so you don't need to remember to post or be present, you can schedule many channels at the same time. Monitor your newsfeeds, flag up searches or keywords, so you can engage with relevant topics.

Look at any existing packages you use to see if they offer integration with one another, to share information so you don't have to enter client details into each one you use. For example, when someone books an appointment with me via Acuity it can add them to my MailChimp email list if they tick the box; it will raise the invoice in Freshbooks and add them to Capsule.

There are also services like Zapier and IFTTT which are much more involved and can be used to create thousands of automated flows for your business even where integration may not be already available.

TAKE ACTION

What three processes in your business would you like to run more efficiently, or spend less time on?

1.

2.

3.

Mumpreneur Case Study ★

Anna Markovits, Markovits Consulting, she has three children, she started the business in 2014.

What does your business do?

Our purpose is to help businesses to be successful by improving their performance through leadership, coaching and people development. We offer business coaching, facilitation, training and consultancy services to businesses of all shapes and sizes, ranging from tiny one-person businesses to global corporates with 50,000+ employees. We work with clients in the areas of management and leadership development, team development, coaching, learning and development consultancy and employee engagement, across the private, public and charity sectors.

What motivated you to start your business?

I have a real passion to enable people to learn, develop and to reach their full potential. Before starting my own business, I was working as a Head of Learning & Development for a government organisation. My role was becoming more and more strategic and policy-focused, and I felt that I was not doing enough of the face to face facilitation and delivery that I really enjoyed. I had received feedback from a number of external consultants that they thought I'd make a really good consultant, and this feedback, along with knowing that I could be my own boss and have a better work/life balance, gave me the confidence to set up my business and leave my old job.

What mistakes did you make when you set up your business?

I took quite a long time to 'make the jump' to setting up my own business, and I was worried that because of the economic climate there may not be enough work out there. In hindsight, I wish I had made the jump sooner! The amount of work I am offered allows me to really assess my ability to help each client to achieve their goals and to ensure I am the right fit for them and their organisation, rather than chasing every possible opportunity. As part of my preparations for setting up my business, I had thought about plans for if there was not enough work, but I hadn't planned for if there was too much – so perhaps I needed to be more optimistic! My biggest challenge was learning how to run a business and understanding the 'rules' and requirements associated with it. This needed to be balanced with ensuring I deliver an excellent service to my clients and invest some time in marketing and networking to enable business growth. I am pretty sure that I have improved my multi-tasking skills in the last couple of years!

How do you juggle family and business?

My four-year-old goes to nursery two or three days a week, so I try and only do two or three days of client-facing work each week, and ensure I have two days to spend with my daughter. When I am busy or have a big project on, this means that sometimes I end up working in the evenings, but I feel I have a really good work/life balance now. I get to pick my older daughter up straight from school two or three days a week, and I don't work in the school holidays, so I get to spend quality time with my children. I am going on maternity leave soon, and I have made arrangements and longer-term plans with some of my clients as to how their work is delivered. I've also got a great network of other people who do similar work to me who I can contract to deliver work for my clients if I need to. Although I will still be running my business while on maternity leave, I feel very much in control and that I am making the decisions, which feels great!

What are your future plans for your business?

I plan to grow my business further once I return from maternity leave. I want to continue working part time while my children are young, and then increase my hours (and the amount of work I can do) once they're all at school. At the moment, I work (through my business) as an associate consultant for some larger consultancies, so some of my clients come through that stream. In the future I plan to increase my number of direct clients and also do some longer-term project work.

Anything else to add?

Remember that people are your greatest asset. Even if your business sells great products and services, it wouldn't be successful without the people who work in it. Be interested in your people, take time to find out what makes them tick and why they come to work, and invest some time in them. Happy employees make better businesses.

Summary of Stage Two

In this stage we have covered:

- The checklist you need to complete to start your business

- We have explored funding and considered how you need to ensure you make a profit

- The chapter on marketing and sales should give you a great starting point for formulating a solid and achievable marketing plan – plus achieve sales!

- We finished on processes and ideas of platforms and apps you can use to make running your business easier

This stage had a lot in it. You might be feeling quite overwhelmed at this point and ready to reach for your CV and be on the brink of contacting recruitment agencies to get a job! But hold on a moment! I never said at any point this was going to be easy, did I?

You might also be worried that you are not making any money and are spending lots of it! Do you know the most common question new business owners ask? How long will it take for my business to become profitable?

You want to know if your risk is going to pay but I cannot give you any clear answer as this depends on the business you have decided to set up. The crux is your costs: the lower these are on a month to month basis, the sooner you will make money. For some it can take three years before they are established and making a reasonable salary; for others it can be within a few months.

Talk to your business adviser and accountant. Make sure you are doing all the things suggested in the book and I mean *all* of them! Make sure you have broken down all the activities you need to do into sizeable chunks to stop you feeling overloaded.

Make a timeline of jobs you need to do – give yourself time limits.

Congratulate yourself on every single achievement and celebrate each success – every day, each week and every month. Every milestone is worth a cheer! From the business ideas, to the logo, to the website launch, to that first customer!

Well done for getting this far – and in our final stage we look at how you can maintain your sanity, grow your business and hear from some more inspiring Mumpreneurs.

STAGE
THREE

Our first two stages were the foundations of your business.
These were the practical steps you needed to take to build your
business. But once the business is up and running, making
money, serving customers, it's important to get some advice on
how to maintain your sanity!

In this stage we also look at growing your business and some
ideas to help you.

Chapter 9

MAINTAINING YOUR BUSINESS AND YOUR SANITY

Outsourcing

Although it might seem most cost-effective to do everything yourself, there comes a time when you need to build a team around you if you are going to be successful, and have time for yourself and your children. You might want to work with a freelancer to take on some of the work you have gained for clients or you might want to work with someone who can help you with your business.

I have a list here of some of the tasks you might want to consider outsourcing.

Bookkeeper and accountant

Getting an accountant or bookkeeper is **important** unless of course you are one. Understanding the complexities of tax is for the experts. I know I save more than I spend on an accountant. I use an online accounting system called Kashflow which interfaces with my website and PayPal. But there are many on the market (see resources) and these do save you time. If you are not going to be transaction heavy or sell online, then an Excel spreadsheet may serve your needs perfectly well.

You must keep receipts and proper records, failure to do so can attract large fines from HMRC. Also, by understanding your income and expenditure you can see where you are making a profit or a loss and make adjustments accordingly.

Virtual assistant

This is a must for many small business owners who want to have time with their family. I found I ended up working into the night, which wasn't practical. So, I used a VA who covered some of those time-consuming admin tasks which enabled me to develop my business. I used a call answering service. Never miss a client's call, they will just call someone else, answerphones are fine, but many people won't leave a message. If you use a call answering service they will answer in your business name, take a message and email or text you. This is far more professional.

Marketing

A marketing plan is essential. You need to have a clear strategy of who you are targeting and how you will target them. If you need help with the marketing of your business, there are many independent marketing consultants who would either help you with a plan and ideas or with implementation or both. However, this can be expensive initially so work through the chapter in this book on marketing ideas and then decide if you need further help. There are many good books and online resources on this. In my view, a good marketing consultant will pay for themselves in the time they save you doing the research and the leads it brings in. A marketing intern or an apprentice may also be able to support you. This means you can concentrate on selling to the leads you have and maintaining the customers' requirements.

Design

Unless you are a designer I would highly recommend you find one, or risk your brochures, leaflets and business cards resembling a school project. You want to showcase your business and look professional, and shoddy design will do you no favours. When you are asked to send out information on your business or give it to customers you want to be proud of it.

Good design is an investment, and this includes your logo. It's a false economy in my view not to get a good, designed brand. Work with a designer who has experience of brand creation and make sure the logo, website and marketing materials are all consistent. Ensure you get the EPS version of your logo and you know the pantone references in case you want to get some promotional goods printed. An EPS version of your logo means you will have a scalable and editable version of your logo. Other file types like JPG, PNG and GIF are pixel-based file formats and therefore cannot be scaled. If you attempt to enlarge a pixel-based image, it will pixelate (the actual pixels that make up the image will become visible). In practical terms, this will lead to your logo appearing blurry, dirty or fuzzy. So, when you get your logo designed ask them to do an EPS version.

Copywriting

Outsourcing your copyrighting makes sense as good writing takes experience and expertise and using someone who has a way with words can really help sell your business. You can use a copywriter to help you for your website and marketing materials. If you work with someone or do it yourself consider the following. You must make sure anyone you work with on your copy for your business is correctly briefed and you give them access to information that will help them write copy that will sell your business for you.

- Use the research you have done in your copy. So, if you know your market well use statistics and information to support what you are writing about.

- Tell a story and illustrate with examples – case studies and testimonials which show how your product or service changed someone's life. This backs up what you are offering.

- Copy first then the headline. More people read the headline than the copy, so you need to make it compelling but write the copy first then the headline will come to you. Make it a headline which will grab attention and make people want to read the article.

- Make paragraphs short and write sentences with impact. Use bullet points to break up the text and sometimes adding quotes can work well to illustrate a point.

- Share expert value – you know loads of great stuff on your topic that others don't so share it. Position yourself as an expert by writing credible information.

- Don't 'we' all over your copy! No one cares about you, they care about what you can do to help them! Avoid overusing this word and also adding loads of cliché statements such as 'we offer great customer service' etc. Focus on what problems you can solve.

- Close off copy with a call to action – what do you want the reader to do?

Website design and SEO

When deciding which web design company to use, do your research. You can generally meet reputable people at networking groups. Also ask other businesspeople you know or Google and then check the companies out thoroughly. Expensive doesn't always mean good, research into the companies you use. Look at their existing portfolio and talk to some of their clients. Ask them questions e.g. Did they listen to the brief, did they complete to time and how helpful were they with ideas? Make sure you give them a good detailed brief. Include examples of websites you like the look of, colours and appearance.

Spend time considering what you need your website to do. What is your website going to be used for? A brochure website simply lists services; an ecommerce site means you can sell your products online.

Check out competitors' websites.

Good SEO (search engine optimisation) is essential to be found, otherwise you will have an expensive showcase and no one will find it. Consult an expert in this, your website company may do this or may know someone.

Your website should be a tool that generates business – it should be working for you!

Important advice for working with freelancers

Having read through the list above of all the jobs you could outsource, you will hopefully have been able to see how much time you can save, and this can be spent on gaining and working with clients that pay you an income!

You could also outsource work to other people in the same field as you, often called associates, and take a commission. This can be an easier route to expanding your business than taking on employed staff. Outsourcing work can be an easy way to grow your business. I asked an expert I met at a networking event, Annabel Kaye, to share some tips with you as this is her area of expertise.

Annabel Kaye supports growing businesses to manage their freelancers. She has been working on the people and contracts side of business since 1980 when she founded Irenicon. In 2007 she founded KoffeeKlatch to support businesses managing freelancers and outsourced workers. She speaks, blogs, writes on this subject to help you get it right – and avoid nasty surprises. Annabel shared some really useful advice as follows.

According to our ongoing survey, there are three reasons why you will want to outsource some of your work to freelancers or other businesses:

1. To get rid of things you don't like to do (admin).

2. To access expertise you don't have (accounting, web design, legal etc.).

3. To expand how much money you can make by getting other people to do what you do and like to do and know how to do (i.e. another therapist, another salesperson).

These outsourcing needs are not all the same, and it is important you know which one you are on. But they do have some key elements in common – and here are Annabel's top tips.

1. Calling people 'self-employed' or 'freelance' does not change their legal status. If they would otherwise be employees, they will still be employees. So, getting someone to come to your office and work for you for 10 hours a week is not going to mean they are 'self-employed'. You can run up some big back tax bills if you don't get on top of this right away.

2. It is not quite as straightforward as employed or self-employed – there is a third category of people – workers. They are people who do work for you personally but are neither employees nor self-employed. They have a full set of worker rights, including paid statutory holidays, discrimination/equality rights and more. Amazon and Uber ran into this problem (along with a lot of other people).

   For more information on the status of people you pay (and how to start figuring it out – see https://www.gov.uk/employment-status)

3. If the people you pay are employees, you must give them a statement of the key terms of their employment (a sort of mini contract).

4. You are not legally obliged to give self-employed people and workers a contract, but you will run into trouble if you don't properly contract with them because:

   a. They own the copyright in what they create for you (if you don't contract for it)

   b. You will need to have some evidence of the arrangement between you to satisfy HMRC if they want to know more

   c. You will want to protect your customer data and be seen to be taking proper steps to do so under data protection legislation

   d. You will want to make sure the people you pay can't take your information (or clients) and set up as rivals, or use your special knowledge for their benefit

5. It is a good idea to set out exactly what you think people are doing for you, by when, to what standard and what is included in the price. That way if you are not both thinking the same thing you can sort it out before you start. Take nothing for granted. Assume nothing.

6. If you can't explain what you want to achieve and how you are going to measure when it is done, it will pay you to take the time before you start paying someone.

7. Freelancers work on results and achievements. Over specifying how a freelancer does something can make it seem that you are their boss (see the employment status test) and if you are buying in expertise this may not be sensible anyway. You can specify security and quality standards – and you should always do so.

8. Work with people who come with experience. You don't have time to train people how to make their skills work for you. But be realistic – they will still need to know what is important to you, and what you value.

9. When asking people who they use (VAs, bookkeepers, web designers etc.) dig deep. Ask them: how much did that cost, what did you do to make that work, what did they do, how long did it take? What is right for one person is not always right for you. Some people are fabulous on big budgets but very cavalier on small ones! Some people are great on small budgets but very unreliable on deadlines.

10. Have a simple contract between you. It will save you so much time and trouble at every stage of the relationship from start to finish.

This is great advice from Annabel and is something you must take on board if you want to avoid problems. Too many people rush into using friends, family and neighbours to help them or find people who aren't really qualified to do the work, which usually ends in disaster! When you do find qualified people, make sure you follow the steps in this book to help, or contact Annabel for more advice. Her details are at the back of this book.

Juggling family commitments around your business

Babies

I juggled a lot during nap times and was very lucky I had a child who slept for two hours during the day and through the night.

- Consider help with household chores, such as ironing and cleaning

- A childminder or nursery for a few hours a week

- Friends or relatives who can help

Pre-schoolers

Playgroups and nurseries can give you the time to work on your business and manage your schedule around that. Use indoor play centres to allow you some time to work while children play or play dates with other children. But this of course depends on the age of your child. You might find they still nap during the day or you can work once they are in bed, which is mostly what I did!

School age 4-16

Once your children are at school you must juggle 13 weeks school holidays a year, as most people do not have a business they can close down completely during these times. If you don't have the support of family, friends or a childminder, holiday clubs and activities can be the answer depending on the age of your child.

It's a juggling act! Here are some ideas that I did so I know they work:

- Use an indoor play area and take your laptop

- Book them into some sports and art clubs during the holidays for a couple of hours a day, mine loved this

- I also took it in turns for play dates with other parents

- I also scheduled in the theme park visits, zoo trips and holidays as this was the reason I worked for myself - to spend fun time with my children.

- So, planning is the key; my school holidays were (and still are) planned and I work around those plans, much like term time, when you do get more time during the day but spend the evenings running about!

Lists and scheduling are vital to make this work.

Schools communicate via email/newsletters and I always diarise the school holiday dates a year ahead. Your county website will list school holiday dates up to two or three years in advance. Also, plan for the plays, sports days, parents' evenings, days out and picnics. Ask the school for dates even if they haven't published to parents – they generally know at the beginning of the school year what they are planning to do. This means you can work around this.

I always planned my working day from 9am to 2.45pm and then again from 8pm although making sure some days I didn't work every single evening. It meant a lot to my children that I was at the school gates and that I was at their school activities, I know this because they told me so!

Support

Parenting groups online: Facebook is a mine of support for parents juggling work and kids. There are tons of groups and if you cannot find one, start one. When I started my business, Facebook didn't exist, so I have to admit I felt quite lonely at times. I think the Mumpreneurs of today have it much easier as there was no networking when I started either.

Your health

I have neglected my health over the years in favour of everything and everyone else. Learn from my mistake and start as you mean to go on. This means scheduling in some time for you. Here are my suggestions and my favourite thing is my regular spa day – I do one a month!

- Massage, reflexology and Reiki

- Beauty and hair salon

- Walks

- Gym or exercise classes

Anything that makes you relax and switch off. If cash is tight speak to the local colleges as they always have offers on beauty treatments with their students or just take yourself upstairs with a good book.

I have also done lots of skill swaps over the years. So, I have had a treatment in exchange for some training or marketing help. I have also been able to review that person and support them by promoting them.

Preserving your sanity and your health is vital; I have seen many people including me burn themselves out trying to do too much. I found running my own business addictive as I wanted to do well not just for me but more importantly for my clients. So, I would always go the extra mile for them and the cost was my own health as I hadn't outsourced enough tasks to be able to rest!

So, before you get run down and unwell really think about this. Running your own business takes commitment as does running a family.

Your business and personal development

I still go on seminars and courses and listen to experts speak. I enjoy being in a learning environment and you can never know all there is to know on everything. I think learning feeds your soul and in turn you become richer in other ways apart from money. So, I think planning in some learning time is vital.

Depending on what you do you may have to do continued professional development (CPD) each year to maintain your qualifications. But even if this is not necessary make a list of some of the skills you need and research courses, seminars, exhibitions that cover this. Your industry will have specific courses and exhibitions but also check more general ones. These events are also great places to network and learn from others. Check the resource list for more information.

Mumpreneur Case Study ★

Julie Grimes, Jaguar White Recruitment – started her recruitment agency in 2011. She has two children aged 12 and 10.

What does your business do?

Recruitment and selection and interview coaching.

What motivated you to start your business?

Lack of quality expertise and service in the industry whilst I worked for recruitment firms, as well as wanting to be part of my children's life. The fulfilment of making a difference to someone's life through my own passion to bring the best out of people, looking for help in supporting them in finding a new job.

What mistakes did you make when you set up your business?

I took whatever I was offered to work on at low price for volume, burnt the candle at both ends and didn't ask for help as I felt like a failure if I needed help.

How do you juggle family and business?

Sometimes I have no idea, but when I think about it I pulled on other school mums for favours at school pick-up and offered help back when I could. I would collect the children and feed them around tea time then work in the evenings when the kids were in bed to keep ahead of the game and deliver what I promised. My husband worked in London from 7am to 7.30pm.

What are your future plans for your business?

To streamline my admin, get help and grow my business with other income streams. I would like an apprentice to train organically to offer the same level of service I do.

Anything else to add?

My advice would be to never give up. Remember the good bits more than the tough times which many of us think about more and beat ourselves up over. Starting my own business was the best thing I ever did, the hardest thing but the most rewarding. I never thought you could be a good mum and have a business, but you can which makes me one very happy person. I won a business award in 2016 and this made all the hard work worthwhile and it was great to be recognised for my achievements in business.

Time management

Time management is such an important skill to learn. I have been hopeless at it, despite trying very hard! So, I didn't feel best qualified to write a chapter on it! I decided to ask someone who I think is one of the best people I know who is amazing at managing her time, Carli Wall from Synergy Business Support. Here are her top tips.

Many Mumpreneurs struggle with time management, simply because we have so much to do and to remember in addition to our work that there is just such a lot to fit into each day. When it comes to keeping your business running, you need to ensure you keep a handle on your essential tasks, otherwise you'll start dropping balls and something will fail. These tips should enable you to manage your time well, and handily they can be applied to any tasks, such as household and family admin, as well as for your business.

- Always **have a to-do list** to keep you focused

Choose a method that suits you. Write it in a notebook, on a whiteboard, or use an app on your phone – all fine as long as you'll use it and update it throughout the day. Start the day creating or reviewing your list, so you can hit the ground running with what needs to be done that day. Be realistic with how many tasks you can get done in that day, and don't forget to carry over anything you couldn't get around to.

- **Prioritise** your workload to ensure the most important things always get done

Always know the most important things that absolutely must get done in your day. Work through your to-do list and prioritise each task depending on if it is **important** (will it directly bring in money for your business or drive your business forward towards an identified goal?) and if it is **urgent** (does it need doing today?).

The highest priority tasks will be important and urgent, try to get these done first as they are vital to your business. Next priority is anything important but not urgent; these will most likely add value to your business but without a tight deadline; allocate some time each day to work on things in this category.

If you have a list of things that are urgent but not important, beware of spending too much time on these tasks. They are most likely responding to interruptions, for example responding to an email or returning a phone call or doing something that has been asked of you by someone else. Their timescales make it urgent, but is it vital that you spend your precious time on it? There's a danger of frustration from feeling like you've been busy but not actually getting anything productive done if you spend too much time on these items.

And what if it's not important and not urgent? This is useful to make you stop and think about what you are taking on and assessing whether you have put it on your list because you feel you ought to be doing it, or because you actually need or want to be doing it. Anything here you can usually delete. If you don't think it's right to take it off your list altogether, you could add it to an ongoing 'wish list' which is separate from your to-do list – things you'd like to do at some point but not actionable right now.

- **Work with your energy cycles**, scheduling heavy work for when you are most productive

If you feel most energetic first thing in the morning, try to get your most taxing jobs done during that time. If you prefer a slower introduction to the day, or suffer from a post-lunch slump, you could use that time to respond to emails and make phone calls as these tasks don't require much energy, but you will still be getting things done. You could do your favourite or most fun tasks at the times when you are least productive.

Some Mumpreneurs find that they can get so much more work done before the family are up in the mornings or after everyone has gone to bed; they can really get their heads in the zone and plough through the work and get so much done, plus there are also fewer interruptions from clients and other people at those times.

- **Check emails at set points through the day,** and only when you have time to action them

The exception is if you truly are waiting for an instruction or urgent reply that must be acted on immediately. If you are simply doing a general check, schedule set times that you will do this, for example: first thing, before lunch, mid-afternoon and at the end of your working day. Checking only at times when you have the ability to respond makes sure you keep the email work batched together and ensures nothing gets missed (like when you check on the move from your mobile phone and think you'll respond later when you get to your desk, and by then have forgotten!).

Process emails according to the following rules: Do, Delegate, Delay, Delete. If it's something you can action or respond to right away, do it right then. If you need to refer it to someone else, do so and let the person know what is happening. If it's something you need some time to think about or look into further before acting on it or making your response, add it to your to do list (and let the person know when to expect some further action or a fuller response). Anything else should be able to be deleted, or at least filed straight away into a folder. Either it's something to be noted and no action needed, or perhaps a newsletter you will save to read at a later time, or plain spam or junk.

- Group meetings and phone calls to **create blocks of uninterrupted work**

One meeting in the middle of the day can waste a whole day by breaking it into two pieces, each too small to do much in. Schedule work like this into blocks if possible, to avoid breaking up the day and interrupting your flow. You could schedule any phone calls you need to make for first thing in the morning, and if you are leaving a message for someone to call you back, be specific about the times you are available by phone. Try to schedule meetings to fit more than one in a day; if you are deciding the venue you could station yourself in one place and have each person come to you, to save your travelling time.

- **Stop multi-tasking**

Working on several things at once can hinder your focus. Many people think they are successful at doing more than one thing at once, but you can achieve more if you focus on one thing at a time, and often in less time too!

- **Schedule breaks** into your day

This will give your day structure instead of taking breaks randomly, or not at all as is the case for many Mumpreneurs. Going too long without a break, whether it's just five minutes away from your screen, a loo or tea break, or a proper lunch break, will mean you start to flag at certain points throughout the day. This will affect your motivation and productivity, and most certainly your output. Scheduling in some time for breaks through your working day will mean you can remain productive in your working time, and get more done overall than if you had ploughed on without any sort of break.

- **Work in sprints** with the Pomodoro technique

This method of time management involves working in intervals of 25 minutes of work followed by a five-minute break. After four rounds of this, take a longer break then start again. Set a timer for each set of 25 minutes and five minutes, so you have an audible reminder of when to stop or start, and during the five-minute break move away from what you were doing (ideal for a tea break or nipping to the loo!).

- **Use your waiting time wisely**

Being a Mumpreneur often means hanging around in the car during school pick-up time, or while your children are at clubs, or you may find you have some time waiting for various appointments or public transport. Use this time productively by catching up with business-related articles, blogs, videos or podcasts that you never usually get round to reading or listening to.

- **Identify your time management obstacles**

If you really struggle to manage your time effectively, and often have tasks hanging over you at the end of the day, try and work out what your obstacles are and overcome them.

Do you have unclear objectives? If you are struggling to stay on track with tasks, get clarification on what you are working on or trying to achieve. Set SMART goals so you have specific actions and timescales.

Is your working environment not working? Could you work better in different surroundings? Maybe you need a dedicated work space at home or to work externally from a shared office or co-working space. Perhaps you would work better with more people around, or even if you could be left alone. You may find you work better with music as background noise, or you might be better off with silence.

Too many interruptions? If you are receiving phone calls, emails or other messages, do they need immediate attention, or can it wait until you have a better time to respond? If you are working from home, are your family members interrupting you or are you doing chores while you should be working? Make sure you leave the chores and chats for when you are not in your 'working hours', and make it clear to people when you are working.

Do you take on too much? If you find yourself always agreeing to get things done and have an inability to say no, you will end up with far too much to do in the time you have available. Don't undertake work you can't complete in the time you have. Understand that you can't do everything, and that some tasks require your attention more than others (see the tip on prioritising). If you feel you really must take on another task, explain when it can be done so there is a realistic expectation set for the timescale, or delegate the job if possible (these things will most likely be urgent but not important).

Do you procrastinate? There are many reasons people give for faffing about rather than getting down to work: "I'll wait until I'm in the mood to do it", "I don't know where to begin", "I work better under pressure so don't need to do it right now" – all meaning you're putting off tasks that you could just be getting on with now.

Maybe you could start with the shorter tasks, or the most urgent, or the more favourable to do for any reason – just start something, anything! Use the Pomodoro technique mentioned earlier and just commit to 25 minutes at a time.

Are you disorganised? Use your to do list to know what you will be working on and be sure to have what you need ready and to hand. Schedule slots in your day for everything that needs to be done. Set reminders in an online calendar or task list to make sure you don't forget things. Make notes when you are having meetings or planning sessions, so you can refer back to them and remember what you agreed to or what you need to take action on.

If all else fails and you really need to get something done – have a Power Hour. Switch off your phone, disconnect from the internet, shut yourself away if possible, and work for one hour solid with no interruptions – you will be surprised how much you can get done!

Mumpreneur Case Study ★

Susan Heaton-Wright. Her business is Viva Live Music. Susan has one son.

What does your business do?

We organise live musical entertainment for corporate and private events in the UK and overseas.

What motivated you to start your business?

I had had a career as a freelance singer and found that this job didn't work well with family life, so I retired. I was already building up a very successful singing teaching practice, teaching from my studio. However, I was often asked to recommend or even arrange live musical entertainment for people (including businesses). It became apparent that this wasn't only a business opportunity but something I knew really well and loved.

What mistakes did you make when you set up your business?

Where do I start! Pricing was one thing: yes, I covered my costs, but I didn't 'cost in' my time. Valuing the service I provide for others and being clear on the price. There is always someone that will deliver a 'service' for less money, but being able to identify the added value of using Viva Live Music was an important lesson to learn. I had to make tough decisions related to the suppliers we used, including a couple who had been ex-work colleagues; once I changed my attitude from 'I am a musician working for musicians' to 'I am a business owner and if you want to work with us, these are our standards', my business was transformed! Learning to delegate tasks that take time, to free my time up to do the things I do best. Not having clear systems in place that made my business run efficiently: once I created these, it was easier!

How do you juggle family and business?

I have a very strict policy of finishing work (when I can) when my son comes home from school and I also cook all fresh food. Now my son is older, very occasionally I am not in when he comes home at 5pm, but food is already prepared for him and my husband. When my son was at primary school I only worked between 9.15am and 2.45pm so I could take him and pick him up from school and be involved in his after-school activities. One thing I learned to do very quickly was not to answer the phone if I was with him because I couldn't give my full attention to the client. For many years, I have had a call minding service – worth its weight in gold. This means that any enquiry is dealt with by a 'team member', rather than the caller being reluctant to leave a message. And I can focus on my family. I also use this when I am on holiday, so the office is never 'closed'.

As to emails, I switch off devices after 6pm and during the holidays I check emails a couple of times a day. As I have a VA, she is able to deal with some things. It is easy to fall into the habit of checking your emails, answering the phone when it isn't convenient (and that doesn't give a good impression) or even feeling you are the only person who can complete a task when in fact delegating or paying for someone else to do something could be a more sensible solution. I also have very clear systems in place for dealing with enquiries, bookings, contracts etc.

What are your future plans for your business?

The business model of Viva Live Music uses freelance specialist support, so I have freelance admin support, tech, accounts, as well as our suppliers (musicians). A new business development/marketing chap is joining us to develop new business relationships within the industry and the aim is to expand this year and next. We are doing more work overseas and have a local representative for the West Midlands to increase our reach in the UK. I am doing more public speaking related to the business too and am raising my profile within the industry which is useful.

Anything else you want to add?

It can be lonely and frustrating running your own business. Don't be afraid to ask other people for advice. Join networking groups where you will get to meet like-minded business owners – particularly networking groups for Mumpreneurs. When you realise that other people are feeling like you and have the same challenges, it makes it easier. Building and running a sustainable business is hard work. It is really easy for the business to take over your time and for your family to suffer – something we don't want! So, set your boundaries. Your business has 'opening hours' just like any other and stick to it! Good luck!

TAKE ACTION

This chapter has covered all the elements you need to consider to manage your business and maintain your sanity.

My advice is to write a check list now of all the points from this chapter that are relevant to you. Think carefully about how you are managing your time and what you can do to create more time for you and your family. Learn how to work more on your business instead of in it!

Chapter 10

GROWING YOUR BUSINESS

I think growing your business revolves around two things: one is the business knowledge you build and the other is growing your confidence. To keep moving forwards you must continually commit to developing yourself, and if you go on to employ a team you need to develop them.

Growing your business will depend on a number of factors, as with young children you may not wish to have a bigger business and may want to stay within the confines of the home rather than renting offices and employing staff – and that is fine.

I often work with people who are in a muddle and have been the victims of their own success. They have too much work and are now working more hours than they were when they were employed! They gave up a 40-hour week to work 80 hours a week, so something is wrong here. They are usually in a mess because they haven't followed the strategy outlined in this book!

So, if that is you I would encourage you to read those chapters and do a business health check. Take a few days to sit down and work through everything you do and how you are doing it. You need to work out how to work smarter not harder and how you can automate your processes as much as possible and maybe take on freelancers or associates to help.

Often the mess occurs because of bad time management; this can be rectified – read the chapter on that in this book.

Like a child, your business will require constant nurturing. It needs consistency, needs reviewing, refreshing and tweaking. If you don't do this, it will begin to fade and head down the road of possible failure.

I know a lot of people who have worked with a business coach or mentor and found that keeps them on track. I have never done that but have been in mastermind groups with other female entrepreneurs and have some accountability to that group. This has helped keep me motivated and on track.

Building your confidence

Lack of confidence is the one thing that I see which holds Mumpreneurs back. This is usually for a number of reasons:

- Time away from the workplace means people often feel out of touch

- Spending a few years brining up a child means you can lose a sense of who you are and what you know

- Fear of failure – running a business can seem daunting and many people lack the confidence to give it a go, worrying it will fail

Whenever I start a new project I always ask myself 'what is the worst thing that can happen?'

When I set up The Best Businesswomen Awards in 2014 I decided to create a UK-wide business award programme to recognise and reward businesswomen. I called a few companies I knew for sponsorship. I could do this because I was well known in my area through networking. They agreed to do it because they knew me, they liked me, and they trusted me! I set up a website, created a brand and decided on the categories – I worked through a process. I booked a launch event and started a social media campaign.

The worst things that could happen:

- No one would turn up at the launch

- No one would enter

But I knew if I worked to a plan using the massive network I had built over many years this should be successful – and it was!

Could this have been so successful back in 2007 – not a chance!

So, you need to know your limitations and decide on the best course of action to succeed. If you work to the ideas in this book, gain advice and research everything, you will build your confidence and your knowledge.

Be prepared to be flexible with your ideas and once you have started your business things will evolve. There will be days when you feel like giving up. People will be a pain in the arse. Your children will be ill or will play up which will stress you out. Your family might be unsupportive or try and undermine your confidence – but don't let them. If you have confidence in your ideas and your business, you will succeed.

Face your fears head on and be positive! Negativity will drown you out, there is always a way to get over obstacles.

"Low self-confidence isn't a life sentence. Self-confidence can be learned, practised, and mastered – just like any other skill. Once you master it, everything in your life will change for the better." Barrie Davenport

Low confidence in my view is caused by negative thoughts. If you are going through a tough time, get to a networking event or meet up with a fellow business owner. The chances are they have experienced the same tough times as you! Talking to others really helps. Share a post in a Facebook group – get ideas and get support.

You need to learn to overcome problems and work through them. When people ask me how I have been in business for so long, I tell them: "I have never let stupid negative people get to me for long! I move on and move up. I try new ideas and if they don't work I modify them. I don't let anything stand in my way and neither should you!"

Sit down once in a while and write a list of what you have achieved. Reading this back is instantly uplifting because it helps us focus on where we are going right rather than the never-ending to-do list. Pin it up somewhere you can see it – this is will pick you up when you feel down.

Mumpreneur Case Study ★

Katie Carr from tommy & lottie shares her story. She started her business in 2014, she has two children.

What does your business do?

We offer modern, unisex baby clothing and prints. Our clothing is manufactured in the UK and is only made from ethically and sustainably sourced fabrics. We offer a good quality capsule baby clothing range which is stylish but practical and comfortable to wear.

What motivated you to start your business?

1. To be there for my kids.

2. Give them experience, inspire them and involve them with the business.

3. Help other people by creating jobs and giving them work experience.

4. I love well-made, good-quality products. Less is more.

5. I had too many ideas that needed something done about them.

What mistakes did you make when you set up your business?

I should have made sure that I did forecasts from the beginning and was realistic about how much it costs to start a business in the market my business is in.

How do you juggle family and business?

It has its days where it is tough to do both, but I would not change it for the world and nothing is perfect. I have time between 9-3 to be as productive as possible so that means planning in advance as much as I can. I write lists daily on what I am going to achieve, yes sometimes the list doesn't always get completed but it definitely helps rather than having no list at all. I have one for family and one for the business and it works for me. I am organised as you have to be and I don't take on too much either, so focus is key.

My two kids are slightly older but that doesn't mean it becomes any easier! In fact, I have less time now than ever, as they go to bed a lot later, homework demands more and they sometimes need support. We have longer conversations about life and the world and this all takes time. I also have a very supportive husband who doesn't interfere unless I ask him to.

What are your future plans for your business?

To grow and evolve and expand the range and launch into other categories when the time is right.

Anything else you want to add?

I believe everything comes down to confidence and self-belief and mindset. If you really want something you can have it, but you have to realise that it takes determination, the ability to deal with failure, having persistence and being positive as much as you can. Knowing your market is very important too so doing research before you start anything is key. Do networking and plan your marketing as without these no one will find you or your product no matter how good you think it may be. But make sure you find what is right for you and fits your business as these take time and cost money. Get a mentor who can help you and do me a favour, ask for help, so many people try to do it all themselves. Not one business in the world became successful by one person.

TAKE ACTION

Growing your business takes action! Ask for help and support and don't rush things.

Write your list of action points you need to consider for growth.

Summary of Stage Three

So, in our final stage we covered how to maintain your sanity and growing your business.

I think it's important to remember everyone has their own business journey which is unique to them. You are the USP of your business. What makes one business in the same industry different from another is the person running it. It is your drive and ambition which will determine the success of your business.

It is your motivation to keep on top of every aspect of your business that will keep you on track. When you lose interest or try and overstretch yourself or become ill your business will suffer.

Each business carries its own unique rewards alongside the risks. Remember to face problems and deal with them – get help! There are always experts willing to support you. Take the time to regularly review everything.

So, having read this book – you might want to ask yourself:

- Is starting and running a business around my family going to be hard work? Yes is the answer

- Will it be time consuming? Yes is the answer

- Will I be sitting on a yacht sipping champagne in St Tropez in five years? Probably not!

- Will I be able to spend more precious time with my children? Yes, if you plan things out correctly.

For most Mumpreneurs you can run a small successful business around your family and earn a reasonable living while raising your children.

I will leave you with a final thought.

Quality

Never sacrifice quality – quality in your goods or services to clients, quality in your business image and quality time with yourself and your family.

MUMPRENEUR STORIES

When I asked on social media for Mumpreneur stories I got tons of replies. I felt this book wouldn't be complete without a range of stories from mums who are running a business now!

I wanted them to share with you their thoughts, tips and views and many of them have echoed my thoughts and reinforced the points I have made.

Here we share some real stories from people who are running a business around their family.

Joanne and Cath from effloresce Ltd. This company was set up by two Mumpreneurs in their early 40s. Joanne has one son aged 10½ and Cath's children are seven, four and she has a stepson aged 13. They started the business in 2015.

What does your business do?

Established in 2015, effloresce was set up to provide startups, SMEs and larger companies with an outsourced team of experts (mostly in the marketing disciplines) to help achieve exponential growth through a combination of strategic marketing initiatives, generating leads, establishing brand presence and driving sales and revenue.

What motivated you to start your business?

Our inspiration was born out of a desire to continue to use our years of learned experience gleaned from our careers, ensuring that all our hard work would continue to genuinely make a positive difference in the commercial world whilst doing that other thing we genuinely love: nurturing our families!

What mistakes did you make when you set up your business?

We like to see the best in people yet one of our downfalls is certainly being too trusting of people when we should have worked with them a little longer (suppliers/other freelancers) to get to know them better first. Strategic brand partnership isn't just for the big boys, it applies at all levels and we allowed our good nature to take over our commercial acumen. Thankfully director level experience enabled us to resolve our 'learnings' and avoid these naive decisions being costly ones!

How do you juggle family and business?

You do learn how to juggle more effectively when you become a mum. So, it's a case of transferring these skills into the world of 'paid for' work. Lists help you to be organised and efficient and ensure every minute counts. Remember why you did this: to have more of a work/life balance and spend quality time with your family. You have to be strict with yourself and switch off. It's tempting to call on the electronic nanny in this day and age, but we pay for that later on so many levels; notwithstanding the guilt! As clinical as it sounds, scheduling time on whatever device you use is a must! Teamwork is also key and it's a fun way of getting the whole family engaged in the cooking, cleaning, tidying and entertaining each other. Having supportive families and a close network is invaluable!

What are your future plans for your business?

To continue to grow the business and work with like-minded people who share our values of honesty, transparency, flexibility and conscientiousness. We won't employ arms and legs! One day an office perhaps, but for now we are able to work virtually with the use of tools such as Slack and Skype, to keep overheads down and make as much profit as we can for the business.

Anything else you want to add?

Our top tips:

- Always remember why you did this; stay true to yourself

- Be organised and efficient; lists are never to be mocked!

- Get out of your house; 21st century working enables us to go anywhere (within school hours!). Work next to a roaring fire in a pub, a garden centre café, a library, a coffee shop, an art gallery – the world is your oyster and inspiration is out there, not just on Google!

- Always believe in your services and your processes and don't lower your standards – ever!

- Know your worth; 'mates rates' are tempting and sometimes a good way to get moving and some case studies on board, but set yourself a goal and a target as to how long or how many of these you need

- Harness the power of networking, both online using social media and face to face, build relationships and ensure your business name is always front of mind

- Gather as many testimonials as possible, via your social network platforms, Google, on your website – they speak volumes

- Running a business is a constant learning curve, absorb as much as you can from free online courses and from your own network

- Learn when and how to switch off completely from work and focus on the family with no distractions

- Surround yourself with like-minded people – team members, suppliers and even clients; be selective – it's your business and to be truly happy, work with people who have the same outlook as you

- If you're not enjoying something, change it; it's your business, enjoy it!

Anna Fontana, founder at My Mini Pinny has two children aged seven and five. She started her business in 2016.

What does your business do?

Makes children's and grown ups' pinnies as well as mummy and me pinny gift sets.

What motivated you to start your business?

I love to sew and I wanted a job that allowed me to be a fully present mum when the children finished their day without my work impacting them.

What mistakes did you make when you set up your business?

I was too modest! I've got a great product that everyone loves, and I was shy about putting myself out there. I still sometimes undersell myself.

How do you juggle family and business?

It's tricky but I try to be strict about only working when the children are at school, so that from their perspective nothing has changed. Doing something for me also makes me a more balanced person, so although I am busier, I am a happier person than I was when there was less to juggle.

What are your future plans for your business?

To be stocked in department stores and more gift shops.

Anything else you want to add?

You'll be surprised how many people you know who can help you succeed. Don't be afraid to ask. From your friend that is a freelance graphic designer to someone you know who is great with a camera. Always be abundantly grateful and they'll be thrilled to help you get off the ground.

Julie Davies founder of Julie Davies Flower workshops, she has one child.

What does your business do?

I'm The Florist That Teaches – I teach women how to arrange flowers. I started my business in 2012.

I don't have a shop. I don't do weddings or funerals. I'm here to pass on the skills and confidence to other women to enable them to arrange flowers for their homes and for special occasions.

I have a partnership agreement with Kent County Council/ Kent Adult Education Services to deliver floristry classes across a number of centres in Kent. I run my own pop-up workshops at fabulous locations in the county – including in recent years at a local flower farm, stately home and farm shop.

Last year I launched FlowerStart – my four-week online flower arranging class, which is specifically aimed at women who can't commit to a regular evening class. Via three emails a week I lead these ladies on a floral journey – opening their eyes to the flowers around them. Each Friday I take them through a hands-on flower arranging project using written instructions, photo-tutorials and video. By the end of the four weeks they'll have had the opportunity to arrange flowers in a straight-side glass vase, in a vintage tea cup and saucer, casually in a jug/vase and to create a tied posy.

What motivated you to start your business?

I retrained as a florist about 12 years ago (in part, in response to being told that I couldn't have children). During and after my training I continued to work full time in my managerial/office-based profession, while taking on occasional weddings and funerals. After my daughter was born I put my floristry skills on hold and out of the blue was asked whether I'd be interested in teaching floristry at Adult Ed. This was perfect timing as my daughter was about to start school. At this point I decided to become Julie Davies Flower Workshops.

What mistakes did you make when you set up your business?

In the early days I allowed my business to be driven by the needs of my customers. I took on wedding and funeral work, which as single/isolated events didn't work commercially for me because as a home-based florist I wasn't enjoying any economies of scale. I was also 'flattered' into joining a formal networking group, which I felt uncomfortable in during the 18 months of my membership. Early morning meetings were hard to juggle with a child at home. And the other members in the group didn't 'get' my business – I wasn't in the business of selling bunches of flowers, because I didn't have a shop to return unsold stock to. Despite the expense, early mornings (and reciprocal migraines), the very formal way of networking did teach me (as a shy girl) the value of networking; and held me accountable for my business.

How do you juggle family and business?

I am really lucky in that my husband is retired. This means that any childcare gaps (and the housework) is a weight taken off my shoulders. Running your own business is a bit like having a love affair – it's all-consuming, and I'm a bit secretive about it, so my family know they are my priority. For a long period of time working at home became quite a 'thing': "Are you on the computer again, Mum?" Or "Why do you have to go out and teach in the evenings/at the weekend?" As I've become more confident in my business (and made the decision not to stress myself out with the deadlines, budgets and expectations of weddings and funerals), and found networking groups that are a better 'fit' for me, I've also been able to spend less time on the computer.

In hindsight I presume that there must be a pattern that all home-based businesses (or new businesses) follow. The high time commitment of the early days, your family feeling second best, you are feeling frustrated that they 'don't get it', to you eventually working out how to balance your responsibilities and commitments.

For me the secret to juggling my family and business is:

- Really honing down my business – I teach, I don't sell flowers.

- Learning to say no – I don't do weddings etc., but I can recommend a great retail/event florist.

- Drilling down to find my USP. Not only that I'm The Florist That Teaches but that I teach online. One of the reasons I gave up hosting my own classes (as opposed to working in partnership on my 'pop-up' workshops) was that I could never hit the right combination of day, time and venue of my classes. I'd book classes on a Tuesday in response to demand and then I'd be told, "Oh, I can't do that Tuesday…" My response was to point these ladies in the direction of other classes locally, until I had my light bulb moment. Why turn these ladies away when I could teach online? They could take a class at a time and place to suit them, anywhere in the world (there's no real time commitment). This was also a lifesaver for me, as I was able to build up my business while being even more 'present' at home. Teaching a two-hour class at a venue takes way more than two hours – plus all the lugging around of heavy boxes of materials.

- Outsourcing jobs – I was really worried that I couldn't afford to pay people to do the jobs that I found difficult/ time consuming. But the pay-back has been amazing. I don't get anxiety attacks when I think about my bookkeeping, I have far more professional images when I work with my photographer, and I don't need to waste hours and hours of my time working through problems on my computer.

- Because I'm time limited I've learned to make best use of the time I have. Scheduling social media at the start of the month, writing a blogging schedule – batch writing blogs. It makes all the difference in terms of stress and saving time in the end.

What are your future plans for your business?

I want to become known as the provider of online flower arranging classes for busy mums.

On the back of having photographs taken for my online classes I've designed a range of greetings cards, which I sell on Etsy – this is a great way of doubling up on the investment in my photographer. As my classes build, this passive income will grow. To develop other online flower arranging courses – spring, summer, autumn, Christmas, weddings.

Anything else you want to add?

You have to keep going. At moments of crisis I remind myself that running my business has been huge for me in terms of personal development. It gives me a role and purpose, and I contribute to the household income. Taking small steps is progress.

Tracy Ross, Blissfully Organised Home Organisation & Decluttering. Tracy started Blissfully Organised in 2011, she has two boys aged 14 and 10.

What does your business do?

I help my lovely clients to get more organised at home or in their workspace which helps give them more energy, saves time and saves money. They can then focus on the more important things in their lives.

What motivated you to start your business?

I worked in marketing for over 20 years for both large and startup organisations, but I had wanted to work for myself for a very long time. Working in marketing requires an organised mind and planning ahead. I guess I am naturally organised and can see the benefits of knowing where to find things at home, dealing with paperwork to be actioned quickly and being one of the main planners in my friendship groups. I also wanted to have a business which has a strong focus on people and supporting them to achieve their goals. I love people and with Blissfully Organised I get to meet a diverse range of people with different needs. It's never dull and I hear some wonderful stories. When you step into someone's knickers drawer you quickly develop a level of trust.

What mistakes did you make when you set up your business?

I think when I started Blissfully Organised I wanted to do everything, but sometimes it was difficult for potential clients to know which service to use. Now I focus on home organisation and decluttering and introduce other services that my clients can use to save time, such as holiday planning, event organisation, errand running and of course marketing. When you run your own small business the lines between work and home life are often merged. Sometimes I'll start working with a client to reorganise their home then find they need advice and support on marketing, so I can offer that too.

How do you juggle family and business?

Working for yourself enables you to have much more flexibility. I ask for help from friends and family when I need it, but I try to balance the jobs where I need to be at a specific location for a fixed time with more consultancy tasks, which has more flexibility.

What are your future plans for your business?

Oh, that's a good question. I offer a discreet and confidential business which is based on the ability to build trust quickly with a client. Expanding the team would seem challenging but I am working on ways that I can offer supportive advice to small groups.

Anything else you want to add?

I would say to anyone thinking about starting your own business that you should definitely go for it. It's an ongoing learning curve but so rewarding when you look back and think I created this from a blank sheet of paper. I would also advise to value your ambassadors – those lovely clients or contacts who continue to recommend you to potential new clients.

RESOURCES

Business networking

Books

Business Networking for Dummies – Stefan Thomas

Instant Networking: The simple way to build your business network and see results in just six months – by Stefan Thomas

Business Networking - The Survival Guide: How to make networking less about stress and more about success – Will Kintish

...and death came third! – Andy Lopata and Peter Roper

Networking companies

www.mumsunltd.co.uk

www.wibn.co.uk

www.theathenanetwork.co.uk

www.4networking.biz

www.bni.co.uk

www.1230.co.uk

www.fabulous-women.co.uk

Websites that list networking events

www.findnetworkingevents.co.uk

www.eventbrite.co.uk

Marketing

Books

All Marketers Are Liars: The Underground Classic That Explains How Marketing Really Works - And Why Authenticity Is the Best Marketing of All – Seth Godin

Marketing For Dummies – Jeanette McMurtry

The Google Checklist: Marketing Edition 2016: SEO, Web Design, Paid Advertising, Social Media, PR – Amen Sharma and Paz Sharma

The Ultimate Small Business Marketing Book – Dee Blick

The 15 Essential Marketing Masterclasses for Your Small Business – Dee Blick

Watertight Marketing: Delivering Long-Term Sales Result – Bryony Thomas

The 1-Page Marketing Plan: Get New Customers, Make More Money, And Stand Out From The Crowd – Allan Dib

Online marketing help

https://www.marketingdonut.co.uk/

Presentation skills

Taming Your Public Speaking Monkeys: A Guide to Confidence Building for Presentations – Dee Clayton

Books about business

The Idea in You – Martin Amor and Alex Pellew

HMRC

https://www.gov.uk/working-for-yourself

https://www.gov.uk/topic/business-tax/self-employed

https://www.gov.uk/set-up-sole-trader

Email

- MailChimp
- Constant Contact
- Dotmailer

CRM

- Hubspot
- Insightly
- Salesforce
- Nutshell

General business support

http://www.greatbusiness.gov.uk/

http://www.fsb.org.uk/

https://www.yourbusinesscommunity.co.uk/

http://www.smarta.com/

http://smallbusiness.co.uk/starting/

www.womenonlyconnected.com

Online accounting

- Xero

- Kashflow

- Sage

- QuickBooks

Social Media Tools and Support

https://moz.com/beginners-guide-to-social-media

www.socialmediaexaminer.com/social-media-marketing-tips-pros/

www.hootsuite.com

www.buffer.com

I would like to thank our generous contributors who shared their business tips and knowledge with you!

Krishma Vaghela www.franchisefutures.co.uk

As a business development professional with nine years' experience in the franchise industry and a mother of two, Krishma Vaghela has spent six years on the operational front leading multiple Pitman Training franchises securing her two Best Businesswomen finalist awards in 2015 and recognition as operating one of the fastest growing franchises within the Pitman Training network. In 2016, Krishma held the position of UK Franchise Sales and Development Manager within a care franchise 'Promedica24' and in 2017 landed a role in London at one of the UK's fastest growing startup tech companies, Laundrapp, where she was the lead for UK development and service provision and managed 35 partners across the country. With proven experience in the franchise space, Krishma also implemented a partner recruitment, training and support programme within the company.

However, in January 2018, Krishma disrupted the franchise consultancy and advisory space when she launched her own business Franchise Futures, with a goal to providing more affordable services to those looking to move into the franchise space and those already operational within it.

Annabel Kaye

Annabel Kaye supports growing businesses manage their freelancers. She has been working on the people and contracts side of business since 1980 when she founded Irenicon. In 2007 she founded KoffeeKlatch to support businesses managing freelancers and outsourced workers. She speaks, blogs, writes on this subject to help you get it right – and avoid nasty surprises.

Using code DG5 on this link you can get 5% off using Annabel's service using this link https://Koffeeklatch.co.uk/Mumpreneur

Carli Wall www.synergysupport.co.uk

Carli Wall is a business consultant working with women who run a business around their family life, helping to develop and improve their businesses. Carli set up her own business when her sons were one and three years old, after being made redundant for the third time. With 12 years' experience in office management and business development, she had already been assisting small businesses outside of her day job, so the logical step was to turn this into a business. Five years later, she has a successful business built mainly on word of mouth referrals and now runs the business with the addition of a baby daughter!

Cheryl Luzet www.wagada.co.uk

Cheryl Luzet is the Managing Director of St. Albans-based boutique digital marketing agency Wagada. She set the business up in September 2011 when she'd come to the end of her maternity leave with her second child and didn't want to go back to her daily London commute. The business has grown from a home-office business focused purely on SEO consultancy, running out of Cheryl's spare room, to a successful and thriving digital marketing agency, employing 11 permanent and 10 freelance staff, managing 45 clients on a monthly basis.

Hannah Miller www.chipperfieldaccounting.co.uk/

Hannah Miller qualified as a chartered accountant and chartered tax adviser at Ernst and Young and previously worked in the tax department at Goldman Sachs in London. Inspired by similar women who had left successful careers to become entrepreneurs, Hannah founded Chipperfield Accounting Ltd in 2013 to enable her to work flexibly around her family.

Chipperfield Accounting is now an established chartered accountancy firm specialising in tax and accounting solutions to a diverse range of clients including individuals, limited companies and sole traders. In addition to bespoke advice, the services include tax planning, limited company accounts and tax returns, personal tax returns, payroll filings, auto-enrolment pension scheme set-up and management, business startup plans, bookkeeping services and VAT returns. Hannah was a finalist in the 2016 Best Businesswomen Awards for Best Businesswoman, Best Woman in Business Services and Most Inspirational Businesswoman.

Many thanks to our Mumpreneurs who so kindly shared their stories in this book.

Bess Sturman – Sturman & Co. Interiors,
www.sturmanco.com

Yuliana Topazly – My Outspace,
www.myoutspace.co.uk

Catherine Firmin – effloresce Ltd,
www.effloresce.co.uk

Leigh Farrer – The Salvage Seller,
www.thesalvageseller.co.uk

Anna Markovits – Markovits Consulting,
www.markovitsconsulting.co.uk

Lorry Edwards – Active Create,
www.active-creative.com

Ravneet Bermi – Puddle Ducks,
www.puddleducks.com

Lara Apoola – HarmonyBooks,
www.harmonybooks.co.uk

Gemma Whates – All by Mama,
www.allbymama.com

Susie Tobias – Wise Genius,
www.wisegenius.co.uk

Katie Carr – tommie & lottie,
www.tommyandlottie.com

Julie Davies – Julie Davies Flower Workshops,
www.juliedaviesflowerworkshops.co.uk

Anna Fontana – My Mini Pinny,
www.myminipinny.co.uk

Tracy Ross – Blissfully Organised,
www.blissfullyorganised.co.uk

Julie Grimes – Jaguar White Recruitment,
www. jaguarwhiterecruitment.co.uk

Susan Heaton-Wright – Viva Live Music,
www.vivalivemusic.com

A special thank you to my group leaders who run amazing Mums UnLtd groups for Mumpreneurs.

Carli Wall – who has contributed to this book. Her knowledge of systems and processes is awe inspiring and has been an amazing support to so many Mumpreneurs.
www.synergysupport.co.uk

Zoe Douthwaite – who has a strength I so admire. After losing her husband when he was just 47 and with her two young children she has moved forward and works alongside me whilst running her own VA business. She supports Mumpreneurs with her humour and encouragement.

Melanie McCarthy – who took my vision and made it possible for the women in her area. She supports them and runs lively informative meetings. She also has a business that is fantastic – a second-hand designer dress boutique. I am always poorer when I visit her.
www.brockhurstboutique.co.uk

Cornelia Raubal – the ultimate networker who worked tirelessly to get her group started and continues to support, inform and inspire.
www.craftport.com

Abby Dennis – one of the most organised people I have ever met. She loves a spreadsheet and we work together on the Watford Expo.
www.watfordexpo.co.uk

Catherine Chapman – a funny and fit gorgeous warm lady who supports her group down in Whitstable.
www.bodyworks-pt.co.uk

I met all these people whilst networking!

On my business journey I have met some fantastic entrepreneurial women and I just wanted to share some of the very best people I really admire. They all took a seed of an idea and have made it grow. Some of these companies might be able to help you to grow your idea!

Dee Clayton – Simply Amazing Training,
www.simplyamazingtraining.co.uk

For help and advice on presentation skills training

Justine Perry – Cariad Marketing,
www. cariadmarketing.com

A marketing agency that covers all aspects of marketing

Jo Wareham – The Little Branding Company,
www.thelittlebrandingcompany.co.uk

For promotional gifts, this really is your one stop shop

June Cory – My Mustard
www.mymustard.co.uk

For help and advice on Google Ad Words and other PPC marketing

And I really want to thank these two ladies for supporting me on my book journey:

Dee Blick – who helped and supported me at the beginning of this book journey www.themarketinggym.org and **Mindy Gibbins-Klein** who helped me to finish it! www.bookmidwife.com

Here is some space for your notes and please do share your journey with me and I wish you luck and every success!

ABOUT THE AUTHOR

I didn't ever consider working for myself. It was never part of my life plan. I was brought up in a working-class family where you got a job when you left school and stuck with it until you retired. There were no entrepreneurial role models in my family. I never sold lemonade on the corner of my street and I would never have dreamt that one day I would own my business and be quite successful at it!

After leaving school at 16 I trained to be a nursery nurse, found I was bored and tried office work. I eventually had a career in the travel industry until I had a baby. I was a single parent from being six months pregnant and I returned to work full time when my son was just 17 weeks old. After trying to juggle childcare and work for two years, mostly unsuccessfully, I relocated back to my home town for support. This was not to be as my dad was diagnosed with dementia. So further responsibility was added to my list: two aged grandparents and two parents who all needed support.

So I had to work for myself, flexibility was what I needed. No employer could provide that. Now I manage a marketing and events agency which includes a networking company for mums in business and a business awards company. I have two boys now aged 23 and 16 and have been through all the problems most mums face and juggled a business alongside it. Plus, I have two rescue dogs which are my joy!

I am passionate about supporting women in business and I hope all the information in this book gives you enough guidance and support to get your business off the ground and running successfully.

I am happy to connect with all my readers, so you will find me on LinkedIn, Facebook and Twitter! Profiles listed below!

Debbie Gilbert

Twitter @VivaDebi @MumsUnLtd @bbwomenawards
Facebook www.facebook.com/mumsunltd

Websites

www.mumsunltd.co.uk
www.viva-networking.co.uk
www.bestbusinesswomenawards.com

Printed in Great Britain
by Amazon